Prison Riot, A True Story of Surviving a Gang
War in Prison
Prison Killers Book 1
By
Glenn Langohr
Copyright © 2011 Glenn Langohr

Prison Riot, A True Story of Surviving a Gang War in
Prison

Published by Glenn Langohr @
www.lockdownpublishing.com

Edited by: Judicious Revisions LLC

~*~*~*~

This book is licensed for your personal enjoyment only.
This book may not be re-sold or given away to other
people. If you would like to share this book with another
person, please purchase an additional copy for each
recipient. If you're reading this book and did not
purchase it, or it was not purchased for your use only,
then please and purchase your own copy. Thank you for
respecting the hard work of this author.

~*~*~*~

You can contact Glenn Langohr via email:
rollcallthebook@gmail.com
Author Page: http://www.amazon.com/-
/e/B00571NY5A
Author Page UK: http://www.amazon.co.uk/-
/e/B00571NY5A
Blog: http://rollcallthebook.blogspot.com/
Smashwords:
http://www.smashwords.com/profile/view/lockdownp
ublishing.com

Facebook Pages:
https://www.facebook.com/glennlangohrcalifornia
https://www.facebook.com/lockdownpublishingdotcom
https://www.facebook.com/KindlePrisonStories
Twitter: https://twitter.com/#!/rollcallthebook

~*~*~*~*

This book is based on true events in the author's life. Some timelines, events, places and names have been changed for dramatic purposes

~*~*~*~

Chapter 1 The Warden Just Arrived

The Warden sat at the oak table and asked Lieutenant Pickler again, "Why are we going to let the inmates' riot if we know its coming?"

Lieutenant Pickler looked at the Warden's name engraved in gold on his chest, M. Parker, and wondered how to explain. Parker never worked at a serious prison. He only worked the soft yards. He might as well have been working at Disneyland. How do I explain to him that when we know the inmates are going to riot we let it happen and get paid time and a half for hazard pay for a while? He explained it a different way…"Warden, all four yards at this prison are headed for war. It's inevitable. The state of California doesn't have the money to shift inmates to other prisons every time we know they're having a beef with each other. Imagine how much money it would cost to ship a thousand inmates to another prison. We'd have to back up a ton of buses. Then, to make room for them at the next prison we'd have to do the same thing. We can't play musical chairs with these scum bags. We have to let them work out their own beefs and if a few die so be it."

Warden Parker knew he was right. He thought about how the Inmate Gang Investigators had received information from a couple of prisoners that the northern Mexicans had orders from their mob shot callers at Pelican Bay. The orders were to regulate the southern Mexicans with a list of living conditions. All the veteran prison guards said the same thing. That the southerners wouldn't bend and a war was going to happen. It was just a matter of when. The Warden got up from the desk and nodded his head. He said, "As long as none of my guards get hurt."

Lieutenant Pickler got up from the table and said, "We have the elite guards on standby for this. We'll contain it when it happens."

Chapter 2 The Domino Riot

Johny Rodriguez looked up from a card game when we walked over and said, "It's going down soon. Can we count on you for help B.J and Giant?"

The other three Mexicans in the card game didn't intrude by looking at us. They kept stoic faces and studied their cards.

I, who answered to the name B.J, thought about my life leading up to this prison problem. This was my third time in a California State Prison, each time for being a drug dealer. This case, the District Attorney went overboard and labeled me a "Cartel level gun and drug dealer". Being a White man who bought drugs from Mexican dealers, the law had it reversed. My first time in prison was at Chino, my second time in prison was at Soledad and now I was in Solano. Now, Giant and I were facing the dilemma of whether to get involved in a prison riot or not.

I looked at Giant. I called him Giant upon meeting him because he looked like that Russian guy Dolph Lungren in the Rocky movie. At 6'8 and shredded with muscle he was my partner in here. I knew he was going to get involved in the riot. He was fond of Johny and some of the others. We played handball and basketball together due to the prison rules as to what courts we shared. We played cards together on tables that were set up as ours inside the building. We used the same showers and in general were allied together. I wanted to set the right example so I said, "There's a way you can count on us."

Johny didn't say anything. He was a stone statue, and still looking at me with his cards close to his chest. The other three Mexicans were now looking at me also.

I said, "If they come running at you on our side of the dayroom or yard, we've got your back."

At every prison in California, every inch of space is fought over. At this prison, inside the building, once outside of the cell, half of the building is controlled by the Black and northern Mexican inmates and the other half is controlled by the White and southern Mexican inmates. That means you can't touch foot in the half that isn't yours. The showers are marked the same way. Even on our own sides of the territories, certain tables and spaces are marked by regular users.

In the building there are two floors we call tiers. The floor has two sides and is filled up with tables and a TV. One side of the floor is for the Black and northern Mexican inmates and the other side is for the White and southern Mexican inmates. On our side the Black inmates control the TV, so we really only have the tables.

Out on the prison yard the Whites and southern Mexicans have even less space. Every inch of territory is marked. You can't stand in the wrong area. You can't walk through the wrong area. You can't sit at the wrong table. It is so regulated that there are certain inmates for a group or race that are stationed to keep watch, almost always in shifts. It felt like what little space we had, was being squeezed tighter.

This prison in northern California has an unusual mix of inmates. Out of the 33 state prisons in California only two are "Hubs" for northern California prisoners. This one and San Quentin are stacked in their favor. The numbers are horrendous. The White inmates make up 10% of the population, the southern Mexicans make up 6%, the northern Mexicans make up 34% and the Black inmates have all the rest minus a small gathering of Asians and Islanders.

For the most part, southern California dominated the landscape of every other prison I'd been too. Cities like Los Angeles, Orange County, San Diego and all the cities that fill the Inland Empire are bigger breeding grounds. The mixture of poverty and an affluent lifestyle seem to breed gangs. Being closer to the Mexican border also plays a factor. At all of those other prisons, the northern Mexicans are short in number and have very little territory. But since this prison was one of the couple that is in their backyard, it is the opposite. The bottom line: at this prison if you are a White or southern Mexican inmate, it's "out of bounds" and you have nothing coming.

Our building on the yard is number 23, and is considered the unofficial headquarters for the yard. We have the biggest cluster of experience mounted up together, but we only have 10 people. Our enemy who declared war on us has 30 people. They also have their most experienced veterans stacked in our building. The other 4 buildings on the yard and the gym have a similar ratio with slightly differing numbers. The gym inmates have it the worst. There are 3 verses 18. The instructions to survive being as outnumbered as we are: to take the initiative in a domino effect. That means as soon as our building "goes off", and all the other buildings see and hear the alarm and watch the building guards run out to get to ours, it's their turn. The motto, handle your business before it gets handled on you.

Chapter 3 The Reason for the War

For the last 36 hours we knew the prison riot was going to happen this morning. During this period I found out that the southerners had infiltrated the northerners to the point that vital information had leaked on one of the other prison yards. The northerners are divided into a handful of powerful gangs but the two that have the most power are the N.S Gang and the N.F Gang. N.S is short for Northern Structure and N.F is short for Northern Familia. Allegedly, they were passing orders to regulate the southern Mexicans by mandating rules to keep them in check. The main rule that wasn't going to fly was that if you were a southern Mexican you couldn't take off your shirt and expose tattoos from L.A or any other southern California city, gang, street, or association. Being forced to keep your shirt on while working out outside was like being told that "You are owned by us and just renting space under our terms." So the defensive-offensive strategy was to be offensive before the northerner's new plan was implemented.

The day before the riot Giant and I walked the prison yard talking to other White inmates about the issue. A sea of inmates dressed in state clothes all looked the same at first glance. Blue state pants with a yellow CDC emblem, along with a blue denim jacket and usually a beanie on top of a head like a helmet, were standard issue. But when you looked closer you could make out all the details that differentiated the races and gangs. While walking I noticed that all the northern Mexicans were more vigilant. They were less active as far as playing card games or even handball and basketball games. There was something in the air and you could feel it.

Each building had a couple of cement tables in front of it. They were six feet long and fit three to four bodies on both sides. Every table we walked by was either a table for Black inmates or a table for northern Mexican inmates. We passed a table for Black inmates who were playing dominoes. It was a heated game and there was a lot of hooting and hollering. One Black man was dressed like a Crip gang member with his pants sagging almost halfway down his legs. Underneath the pants he had three pairs of white boxer shorts all sagging at different levels. His hair hung in Snoop Dog style braids and his big puckered lips were flapping with all the crap he was talking. He had a domino in his hand and was jabbing it toward the table and then finally slammed it. The domino spun in circles and he placed it and screamed, "Booyaa!"

The next table was a northern Mexican table. Eight convicts were stationed. A few were sitting on the table. I noticed two of them were positioned to look at the gun tower and two were positioned to look at the yard. The rest were looking in every other direction. They differed from the southern Mexicans in one distinct way. They were missing their culture. They didn't act Mexican. Most of them acted like they were Black gangsters. Some of them even did their hair in corn rows or other Black hair styles. They always studied the yard and people that walked by on the verge of glaring at them in a mad dog style. Giant and I got an extra serving of it for playing sports and cards with the southerners.

At each northern table we passed it felt the same way, like they were starting the war with their eyes. It was the wrong way to go about it. Secrecy always wins the first round.

Being as outnumbered as we were, the White inmates didn't have a table on the yard. We shared one with the southern Mexicans and they only had one. Most of the White inmates on the yard didn't even use the table. We walked past it and found the White convict we were looking for in his usual place. He was standing by our building doing his normal workout. We watched his six foot two frame drop to the ground for a set of pushups and then his big bald head popped back up. He lifted one knee to his chest and then the other one. His hands swung out and both fists hit his stomach to complete the repetition. The next repetition started by dropping for another set of five pushups. We stood off to the side and watched while waiting for him to give us a moment.

I thought about what I knew about the convict besides the fact he was doing a life sentence and was from Stockton, California. He went by "Dog" and probably had the most influence for the White race on the yard. At fifty years old and with a calm demeanor, he was very approachable. Though he was found guilty of a double murder over twenty years ago he was now a model inmate who was doing everything is his power to build up positive credentials. He practiced yoga and other meditative therapy and wasn't allowing his prison time to do him. I admired his fortitude. I gave him a nod and said, "We want to talk to you when you finish."

Dog scrunched up his face a little and tilted his head back in a convict look and I realized that as hard as he tried, it was impossible not to be influenced by prison life. I knew that he didn't like to get involved in politics but at the same time wanted a healthy amount of influence on the yard. It was only natural and a survival trait to not want the winds of other people's influences to force you into things you didn't want to do. It was apparent that Dog didn't like our influence. When I first got to the yard I didn't like the fact that the White inmates didn't have a table on the yard. I didn't like the fact that we didn't have any control of a TV in the building. The Black inmates controlled the TV on our side of the dayroom and that squeezed off what little space we had even tighter. They turned the volume way to loud for TV shows like Jerry Springer, early in the morning. One morning it got on my nerves so much that I broke tradition. I walked right up to the TV I wasn't supposed to touch in front of over twenty Black convicts and turned it down while saying, "Have some respect and keep the volume down in the morning!" Dog hadn't appreciated it. The Black inmates went to him to set me straight, that the TV was theirs and we weren't to touch it. During the conversation with Dog he inferred that I was instigating a problem and I inferred that he was acting like he was more loyal to the Black inmates then his own. At the time, the southern Mexicans were ready to go to war with me against the Blacks and Dog didn't like it. It gave me too much power.

Now, Dog knew the riot was coming, but he didn't know when. We weren't here to tell him. After a patient fifteen minutes of waiting, Dog finished his workout and gave us the nod. We walked closer and I started the conversation. "Hey brother, what do you think of this war brewing?"

Dog took a deep breath and wiped the sweat from his forehead with a towel. He looked at me in the eyes and said, "I hope they kill each other, should be fun to watch."

I knew that the southerners didn't trust Dog, or hardly anyone else enough reveal their morning plans. Dog could be to close to a northerner from growing up in the area or doing time with one. I didn't expect his response though. I asked, "What if the northerners run into our territory to attack the southerners? Are you okay with that?"

Dog said, "I'm fine with that."

That was hard to understand. We had rules about territories for a reason but he wasn't willing to enforce what little we had.

Giant grunted and lost his temper. He didn't like Dog. He didn't respect how willing he was to put up with so little respect, yet want it. He said, "I'm helping the southerners."

I stuck to my earlier diplomatic decision. "Dog the Whites and southerners don't have a TV in the building or hardly any space to congregate. What little we have I'm protecting. If the northerners jump the southerners in our territory I'm lending a hand."

Chapter 4 The First Domino to Fall the Following Morning

The three Mexicans from southern California walked to the chow hall from the gym. By their A.K.A's it went: Dreamer from South Los Angeles, along with Travieso and Bugsy- both from East Los Angeles. Dreamer was getting up in age for this kind of stuff at 50 years old. Both Travieso and Bugsy were youngsters at 18 years old. With Dreamer leading the way, they kept an eye on the northerners about 20 inmates ahead of them in line. There were 15 of them in a row and even though all the inmates wore the same blue pants, they wore theirs hanging beneath their asses. Besides the falling off pants, some of them walked with an exaggerated limp like they were trying to hard. It was a kind of swagger pimp walk that said I'm the big dog.

Entering the chow hall, Dreamer's eyes worked hard to determine which seats they would all end up in. The chow hall had rows of metal tables and there were eight tables per row. Each table had four metal chairs attached. The inmates had to get their chow and stay in line and fill up each table. Scanning the area it was easy to see ahead to where inmates were going to have to sit. The northerners were going to get split up. Dreamer watched 4 northerners sit at the end of a row and all the rest walk 40 feet away to the first table in the next row. They were separated by 7 tables, so far, so good.

Dreamer scanned the entire chow hall to see where the prison guards were stationed. There were six prison guards spread out. There was one on each corner and two in the middle of the tables. They were keeping an eye on the inmates to make sure they didn't try to sit out of their place in line. There were two guards above on a steel catwalk like tower. One held a rifle and the other a block gun. Both were studying the inmates. While Dreamer got his plate of food from an inmate who worked serving it, he was relieved that the seating was going to work out perfectly.

Dreamer, Bugsy and Travieso walked with their trays of food and got a table across from the four northerners at the end of the row. At first they pretended to eat. Then, Dreamer got up and took flight. He unleashed a barrage of punches. The unaware northerner he picked was in the middle of eating with his back to Dreamer. He went down for a second. The other three northerners flung themselves at Dreamer with fist flying. Inmates at other tables recoiled as if they were under attack. The alarm went off.

Bugsy and Travieso each had a homemade prison knife. Pieces of steel that had been cut from the gym lockers that inmates used worked well. In their case, they didn't have the time or skill to fashion them into deadly weapons. The dull steel was ineffective but did the job. After a few pokes the unsharpened weapons bit into too much flesh and flew out of both youngster's hands and it was an old fashioned fist fight.

The northerners at the table fought back valiantly and got the battle to even minus the blood from the bad start. By the time the rest of the northerners in the other row realized what was happening, it was too late. The prison guards closed in and others were on the way from the buildings. The prison guard in the tower fired two rounds from two separate block guns and gave the warning, "Live rounds coming next!"

That and the pepper spray from the nearby guards got the 7 fighting inmates to dive to the ground away from each other. One by one, prison guards secured each combatant with zip ties. Other prison guards showed up from other buildings on the yard to secure the perimeter even further and await orders.

Chapter 5 We're Next

We left our building in an armed escort to the chow hall for breakfast. That meant there were 3 building guards stationed on the floor holding block guns studying us. They ushered us into a line just before the entrance to the vestibule underneath the gun tower. I looked up at the guard in the tower. He was extra vigilant and holding his rifle in his hands. On the other side of the 20 foot long corridor we only made it a few feet before the alarm went off. Everyone's attention went to the chow hall where a red light flashed on top. Inmates in line began to get down on the ground. First in a crouch, and then all the way down. I stayed in a crouch. I turned like that, and looked up at the tower guard. He was hearing what was happening on his radio. By his heightened reactions, we knew it was on. We knew it was the gym inmates who were in the chow hall. This plan was set up to rescue them out of harms way first.

We were ordered to get on the ground and the adrenaline jack hammered through my veins harder with the noise.

"Get down! Get down!" The gun tower guard screamed through speakers that temporarily drowned out the noise of the alarm. The alarm sent a screeching and whining sound of decibels that rose and fell, over and over.

In the chow hall about 200 feet away from our building we heard the sound of block guns echoing, "Boom! Boom!Boom!", and more yelling by guards in the fight, "Down! Down! Down!"

We watched the building guards we passed in our building finally come out holding block guns and rifles in the air. Their uniforms were bogged down with gear. Pepper spray canisters the size of small fire extinguishers rattled on one side and on the other batons banged around as they ran toward the chow hall.

We watched the same thing happening in the other buildings. One vestibule door after another screeched open and guards came pouring out. They were going to be running all morning chasing dominoes. Above each vestibule a gun tower guard held a gun halfway out an open Plexiglas window.

By the time the guards got to the chow hall the action seemed to be over. But the guards weren't coming back. That told us it was for real. If it had just been a couple of random people fighting they would have turned around. The tension level went up a notch.

We waited on the ground and those of us who knew what was coming were more ready to jump up if necessary. Instead of looking at the chow hall, some of us started looking at the inmates around us. I found a couple of our known enemy lying flat on their stomach's 10 feet away. The way they were studying the chow hall told me they hadn't detected anything yet.

Time seemed to slow down. It felt like with each second that passed, anticipation increased, and so did something else, awareness. The natural born instinct to survive and protect wasn't at the same level for all of the inmates. Those who had grown up through more adversity recognized those who hadn't lived on the razor's edge yet. It was all the study of body language.

I saw awareness dawn on our enemy. They weren't looking at the chow hall anymore either. They knew it wasn't just a random fight. They both looked right at me. I was caught staring right at them. I played it off like I was in the middle of looking up at the guard in the tower and turned my head. I still had them in my view out of the corner of my eye. They were whispering to each other. Their lying bodies arched up slightly and they were much more ready to jump up.

The guard above us in the tower was like a statue staring at the chow hall and all of us below at the same time. I saw him react to a call he was receiving in his headset. His head nodded and he replied. Then he looked straight down at us while the other tower guard got on the microphone and announced, "Get back into the building. Chow is coming to you this morning."

That signified that the business in the chow hall was either a stabbing or riot. I heard the vestibule door 10 feet away screech and rattle open on rollers and studied the line of inmates in front of me. One by one, inmates were told to get to their feet by guards who were now coming out of the chow hall. We popped back up to our feet and walked back into the vestibule.

As I walked through the tunnel I realized there were 2 enemies inside with us. It would have been the perfect time to attack. It would have been hard for the guards to see who started it. Also, it would have protected us from getting caught on the wrong end of a 15 on 2 blood battle. There was only so much space.

I couldn't do it; the orders were to wait until we were back inside the building. As I walked the last few paces through the vestibule tunnel my adrenaline shot through my body so hard it demanded a reaction.

I got back into the building and didn't know what to do. I didn't want to be the one to "kick it off" in our building. I was just here to help. But the problem I understood intimately was that if I didn't give my adrenaline a release soon, the spike of energy would fall and paralyze me into inaction. It already felt like a balloon inside of me popped, and my body wanted to melt.

My steps were getting heavier and it felt like I was pulling them out of wet cement. I made it 15 feet into the building and was heading for the stairs on the right side when I turned my head. It felt like I was underwater as my neck slowly turned and my lower body slowly pivoted. Other inmates were walking a little faster and most were going back to their cells. Not the Mexicans. The northern Mexicans were grouping up about 20 feet from the vestibule opening. The southern Mexicans were playing it off like I was. I looked for Giant. He was starting up the stairs in the middle of the building about 60 feet away. I turned back around and started up my stairs.

Before chow I stashed a weapon 20 feet from the stairs in a trash can. It was one of the easiest and fastest weapons to make in prison and didn't take much skill. As I got to the top of the stairs I turned again to look. There were 30 northern Mexicans grouped up around the middle of the building and I was surprised the guards weren't demanding them to lock it up in their cells. I looked for Johny and found him. I started getting worried about him being all alone and wondered why all the southern Mexicans weren't clumped up together as well. Johny was walking toward the stairs I just climbed and I saw who he was meeting, another older southern Mexican from L.A who went by Wino.

I walked to the trash can against the wall and pulled back the plastic trash bag and dug my hand down the edge of it. I felt what I was looking for, a sock with a can of beans in it. Before pulling it out I looked at the gun tower. He was the only one who would be able to see what I was doing that I had to worry about. His attention was on the sea of northern Mexicans, now on the move, coming right toward Johny and Wino.

With my back to the gun tower, I quickly fashioned my weapon down the waist of my pants so that the end with the beans in it was tucked. The rest of the sock spilled outside the waist of my pants for easy access. I walked toward the stairs just in time.

Below, the northern Mexicans split into 3 obvious groups. Their shot caller for the yard and his right hand man walked directly to Johny and Wino, a second group splintered off on the left and a third group splintered off on the right. As I got to the stairs and took one step down they were already squeezing in on them.

I heard Johny ask, "Do you want to talk about this?"

The shot caller for the northern Mexicans didn't answer. Instead he fired a right handed bomb of a punch from the hip. It caught Johny flush in the side of the face and I watched while I ran down the stairs. Johny's lanky frame lifted in the air sideways in a sweeping arc. He managed to land on his right foot and plant. My feet were running so fast down the stairs that at the half way point it felt safer to jump all the way down.

I landed hard and noisy and crumpled a little. I gathered myself and turned toward the onslaught. Twenty feet in front of me was a wall of running northern Mexicans. It was like the movie Brave Heart. Everyone was yelling war sounds as the action met more action. I yanked out my sock and wrapped my hand around it so that the can of beans was only 9 inches away from my wrist. I didn't want the arc to be so long it bounced back into my face.

I passed Johny and Wino in a blur just as the outside group of northern Mexicans got there. There were 10 bodies in a rushing wall. In my hurry to block off that front I was off balance. I whipped my can of beans at the tsunami of rushing inmates. It was ineffective. The force of too many people lifted me in the air and I almost panicked at the loss of control. It felt like I was being tackled in a foot ball game where the defenders kept the runner in the air to attack the ball to force a fumble. Floating in the air I spun my body and it kept me from getting absolutely dumped on my head. Instead, I rolled with their momentum by leaning into it until my back was against other bodies. I was able to land on my feet in a crouch and popped up and turned. I no longer had my worthless weapon. I fired right left combinations as straight and fast as I could and felt myself getting surrounded. Punches from all sides were landing and I heard them cracking the side of my head and face. In the midst of so many attackers I couldn't see. That fear kicked in another serving of adrenaline and I responded by running like a football player into bodies. It worked and cleared enough space. I turned toward my attackers and looked to see how Johny and Wino were doing.

There was blood everywhere. I saw it on the floor and on the wall and began to hear the alarm that had been going the whole time. I heard the guard in the tower screaming into his microphone. "GET DOWN! GET DOWN!" I heard block guns from the tower and closer on the ground echoing throughout the building, "BOOM!! BOOM!! BOOM!!" Next, the guard in the tower heaved out canisters of tear gas. It sounded like air coming out of a tire as it leaked noxious gas. My eyes started burning and I felt it burning in my chest.

My view filled up with attackers again and firing punches protected me. Without being squeezed in by so many attackers I backed two northern Mexicans up with more powerful punches. I felt someone bump into my back from behind and turned in a blur with my arms above my face. It was Giant.

The prison guards that ran by sent pepper spray everywhere like a hose and I felt it blast against my face. I turned away from it and kept fighting until I saw most of the other inmates beginning to get down. Slowly, one after another, inmates put their hands on the ground and then their knees and then finally began to lie all the way down on their stomachs. I began to realize how drastic this riot was in places.

I found Johny about 20 feet from where all the blood was and wondered how in the hell it got there. He wasn't bleeding, and it didn't look like any of the other southern Mexicans were. When I looked at him from the stairs he wasn't holding a weapon. Maybe Wino had one, or a number of the other southern Mexicans. They had all made it and were on the ground clumped together next to Johny and Wino.

I found the northern shot caller. His once white T-shirt was soaked with dark red blood from the neck down. It was pouring onto the floor. His face looked pale. He looked like he was about to pass out. Right next to him, another northern Mexican was bleeding from his side and neck. I looked closer at his neck and saw an artery pulsating dark red blood in squirts onto the floor. His face looked pale. He passed out.

I felt a baton whip across my body and another stream of pepper spray blasted into the side of my face. I realized I was the last one standing and had prison guards all around me yelling, "GET DOWN! GET DOWN!"

I lowered myself to the ground in compliance and did a quick 360 degree look around to make sure I knew where the closest enemy was. While I scanned the perimeter I realized that the next building of the domino was going at it. Both tower guards reacted to the info. The one holding a gun out the window looked that way. The one at the microphone yelled the info into the speakers. By the sound of his voice, it was obvious they knew they lost control of the prison.

Our building had over 40 prison guards in it. That meant that every other building didn't have any guards in them, except for the tower guards. I imagined what was happening in the next building. The tower guards were watching the inmates war beneath them unhindered. The only thing they could do was yell into the microphone and shoot at them.

It looked like the prison guards were in over their heads. They all looked at each other questioning what to do. Run to the next building to quell the riot or stay in our building to keep our riot from going off again? After a little hesitation some of the older prison guards figured out what to do and started barking orders. A number of guards stayed in our building and the rest ran out.

Chapter 6 The Next Domino to Fall

The southern Mexicans looked at each other waiting for someone to take the lead. Topo was the oldest at 48 years old, and by reputation, had the most to lose if his building didn't respond. While all the other inmates in the building started to get down in a crouch from the second alarm, Topo ran for the northerners. He found the tallest one at well over 6 feet. At 5 foot 2 he looked like a little monkey as he jumped in the air and used his left arm to hook around his adversary's neck. Hanging on with one arm, Topo's right hand flashed a piece of steel in and out of the northerner's side.

The other 7 southern Mexicans followed Topo's lead. They ran at over 20 northerners and a few of them ran away. Then, they seemed to realize they had the southerners outnumbered and stayed and fought. The battle raged without the interference of any prison guards.

In the gun tower, the two prison guards watched in disbelief. Neither had ever seen an organized riot of this nature. Both guards grabbed block guns and fired at the rioting inmates 60 feet away. The blocks ripped through the air and bounced off the backs of inmates without noticeable effect. The shots came from to far away, at further than 40 feet the compacted wooden blocks lost speed with the lack of aerodynamic structure. At that distance it was the echoing "BOOM!" that had an effect. The blocks lay harmlessly on the ground in pieces burning on fire while the inmates continued to unleash on each other.

The tall northerner tried to use his hands to pry Topo from his neck. In a panic, feeling his body being repeatedly punctured, he swung wildly and Topo went flying through the air, still holding his piece of steel in his right hand. He landed on his feet and immediately got back into the action.

The northerners began to turn the tide and started to circle the southerners. Topo came in from the outside edge and whipped his knife hand through the air at scattering northerners who realized they were outgunned by the weapon.

The noise from the vestibule door creaking open scattered the warring inmates even further. Prison guards poured through the tunnel into the building and let loose a fresh round of block gun rounds. Much closer than the gun tower, these shots were effective. One bounced off a southerner's head that was still fighting and he was thrown to the ground by the force. Another southerner still fighting took a wooden projectile in his back and went down coughing to get air.

Other prison guards fanned out and sprayed enormous amounts of pepper spray and drenched inmates in an orange haze. Everyone dove to the ground and began spreading out from each other. The tall northern inmate who had carried Topo on his back was leaking blood out of the side of his shirt. It was pooling up on the ground and he seemed to just notice it.

Chapter 7 Murder or Self Defense?

We heard the sound of block guns going off in the next building and all the same ineffective orders from guards to "Get down!" Over and over it went until it seemed to die down like our building had. Then we heard that building's vestibule door screeching back open as the guards ran to the next building as that domino fell.

I looked at Giant's shocked face and realized this was the first real riot for him. He was studying the injured northern Mexicans and said, "It looks like those two are dying."

I looked over there. He was right. The shot caller was even paler and his eyes were fluttering like he was barely holding on to consciousness. The other one with the head and neck wounds was lying on his side and the pool of blood on the floor was getting bigger. The blood was running down the floor and other inmates who were lying down tried to move out of the way. Eight prison guards were stationed in the area and a couple of them lifted their batons in the air and yelled, "Stay down. Don't move!"

The inmates quickly dove back down and let the blood soak into their clothes.

The vestibule door to our building screeched open and I looked up at the gun tower. One of the guards was stationed at the window overlooking the yard and he was looking right below him at whoever was on their way into our building. The other guard in the tower was at the control booth opening the second vestibule door entrance to the inside of the building.

We saw the medics enter wearing white uniforms in contrast to the guard's green uniforms. They ran past us right to the dying inmates. One of the medics lifted up the shot caller and began to pull off his once white T-shirt. The medic motioned for help and another medic lifted up an arm as the shirt climbed up enough to get it all the way off. I counted six stab wounds and again wondered who had the weapon. The stab wounds started at the lower stomach and climbed up the chest. They were clean lines about an inch and a half long. Whatever weapon was used was a good one. There weren't any jagged marks and they were deep puncture wounds.

The shot caller's legs were starting to buckle and the medics held him. Another medic packed each stab wound with gauze while another medic walked white tape around his whole body like he was a mummy. After two minutes of wrapping him up they laid him back on the ground and rushed to the other unconscious man. One of the medics had his fingers pinched to his neck to cut off the blood flow to the carotid artery. Another medic was feeling for a pulse. He nodded to the other medic that he found one.

Other medics ran through the vestibule door carrying sleds. They ran to the two critical inmates and the process to get them into the sleds began. Four medics positioned themselves around the body and lifted and slid the inmate onto the first sled. From there they strapped in his ankles and waist so he was locked in. Then they went to the next inmate and did the same thing. The sleds were stationed on wheels and folded up to about waist high. We watched both sleds run past us through the vestibule door.

The sound of a helicopter landing nearby magnified the level of the riot and I realized there were going to be casualties. My mind was having a hard time taking it all in. I just couldn't fathom this level of riot either.

Chapter 8The trip to the hole.

After the medics were cleared out of the building another army of prison guards poured in. For the next 20 minutes every inmate was kneeled on, stepped on and pinched into position to accept zip ties to wrists painfully yanked behind backs. We were ordered from the tower to stay lying on our stomachs in the prone position. Some of the inmates looked like bananas they were so arched up.

The army of new prison guards left the building on their way to the next one. I realized they were dressed a little bit different. Their uniforms were a darker green and they had stitching on their chests and shoulders to signify they were from an elite unit. I'd heard there were special facilities stationed between California prisons that housed units like these.

I knew we were going to Administrative Segregation, also known as "The Hole", "Super Max", or the "SHU", the-Security Housing Unit. With over 100 inmates involved in the riot, this was going to take all day. My hands behind my back were already straining my shoulders at an unnatural angle. The only thing to do was try to find the best angle to lay, sit or stand during the process. A process I was scared would last all day.

I studied Giant on the ground next to me. His long arms were better able to handle being behind his back. He asked me, "Do you think any other Whites helped in any of the other buildings?"

I knew Giant already knew the answer to that. We had been having talks with other White inmates about this riot. They didn't want to get involved. I shook my head and said, "Nope."

The only possibility was another White man in the next building who went by Danny-Boy. He was from LA and knew it wasn't honorable by our standards to allow an enemy to run into our territory against an ally. He had said he was on the fence and might help.

Giant asked, "How long do you think it will take for us to get housed in the hole?"

I was way to optimistic with my answer. "At least six hours."

Six hours later we were still in our building. The prison guards had moved the twenty northerners to the other side of the dayroom. The side they should have stayed on. My shoulders were screaming in pain from the unnatural angle. I felt like screaming to off set the pain and I was moaning and moving all over the place trying to find comfort. My mind was replaying the riot over and over in my mind's eye. I was trying to imagine what happened to the two northern Mexicans that might be dead by now. Who stabbed them with such a deadly weapon? I kept rehearing the sound of the helicopters. My mind's eye kept replaying the two northerners being run out of the building on stretchers. How they were unconscious. Also, I tried to imagine how Giant got down the stairs and made it to me so I asked. "How did you find me through all of those fighting inmates?"

Giant smiled at me and said, "I'm taller then all the rest. I had to fight my way to you though."

Giant explained how a couple of the northerners tried to attack him but that with his longer reach and fighting experience they couldn't do anything. We both constantly moved and shifted to a temporary position of comfort that ran out fast. Other inmates were no longer lying on their stomachs. Most were sitting.

I looked at the wall just beneath the gun tower. In red letters it said, NO WARNING SHOTS. It was a lucky thing that the gun tower didn't fire any live rounds. They were able to shoot lethal rounds when weapons were being used. I hadn't seen any either. The whole deal was like magic.

Finally, we heard the vestibule door creaking and shaking as it opened. The army of elite prison guards poured through walking on their toes like they were all amped up and ready to proceed. They started with our side of the dayroom. Their strategy was to get the outnumbered group to the hole first. It made sense for security reasons. The last few prison guards came in with crime scene kits and cameras. We watched them tape off almost the entire dayroom. The cameras came out and the lights started flashing. The area where the fight had started had a pool of blood about six feet long and a couple feet wide. A prison guard pulled out a flash card and placed it next to a weapon he'd found. Another guard said, "Here's the other half of it."

The guard in the gun tower was studying the scene below. He asked, "What kind of weapon is that?"

The guard looked up at him and said, "It was a pair of barber scissors. It looks like they took them apart and created two deadly weapons."

The guard in the tower nodded his head and said, "Deadly alright...Inmate Hugo died before they made it to the hospital."

The prison guard on the ground whistled and asked, "How's the other one?"

The tower guard responded, "He's still critical with a punctured lung. There's another inmate from the next building in the same condition."

I looked at Johny and Wino. They were sitting on the floor at an angle leaning back with their hands zipped behind their backs. Both were looking at the ground. It felt eerie, like I was somehow getting them in even more trouble by looking at them. I noticed Giant was looking also and we both turned our heads at the same time. All the rest of the southerners were looking in Johny's direction to see his expression. One by one everyone mimicked him and looked at the ground.

A few minutes later we saw another, cruder weapon found. It looked like it was made out of melted plastic. The guards found a few more crude weapons and listed them into evidence.

One by one we were lifted to our feet and ushered into a line in front of the vestibule tunnel. I felt the pepper spray on the side of my body start to reignite and as it mixed with sweat it sent a burning vapor back into my eyes and throat. When our line was complete with all 10 of us we were ushered through the tunnel. At the end of the tunnel the sunlight was like more kerosene to the pepper spray and a fresh wave of burning hit me.

The prison yard felt like a ghost town. Instead of the regular pulse of normal activity there was deadness to it. Like everything was in slow motion and nothing was going to happen for a while. We were escorted 40 feet and then forced to sit down. The procession in front of us, on the way to the hole was what was keeping us. The buildings behind us in the order of involvement in the riot were waiting on us.

Movement flashed out of the corner of my vision and I looked on top of one of the buildings. Two prison guards were stationed with rifles. I looked closer, it was the elite guards. While I told Giant I found a couple more on another building. They were on top of every building on the yard. It was eerie. Like the military was taking back the prison.

We were lifted back up to our feet and the procession moved forward. Another hundred feet later and we were back on the ground. The pain in my shoulders was almost unbearable. Screams and grunts were starting to come out of my mouth with regularity. Other inmates who were in pain asked the prison guards to remove or loosen the zip ties. The guards all had the same response, "Not going to happen."

For a grueling 13 more hours we moved slowly toward the hole. The prison guards who were escorting us didn't seem to have emotions. They were all so calloused. It felt like they were getting pleasure from our extreme pain and agonized faces.

When we finally made it to the hole I realized why it had taken so long. We were being housed in the building right next to the hole. There were so many of us that we didn't all fit in the regular hole. The building we were entering had to be emptied of inmates for us to fit. Listening to the guards we found out the other inmates had been scattered to all of the other prison yards. My mind was becoming void to anything else other then getting my hands released.

Finally we stood in front of our new cell on the bottom tier. It was a heavy steel door painted green with a tray slot about halfway up. The prison guards holding us by our zip tied arms yelled at the tower guard, "Pop cell 107!"

We stepped into our new cell and heard it close behind us with a resounding thud. Giant let me back up to the cell door first. I heard the key enter the tray slot and the noise of it folding down. I pushed my zip tied hands through and felt the plastic ties cut loose. My shoulders were so numb they felt dead. I couldn't lift my arms an inch. It felt like they were paralyzed.

The bunk beds were sheet metal and I asked Giant, "Can I start off on the bottom bunk?"

He said, "Sure. Go ahead."

I crawled on the bunk. There was an ultra thin and tore up mat on it. I didn't care. It felt like the ultimate freedom to be able to let my arms lay at the side of my body after almost 24 hours. My shoulder sockets felt fried, like they would never be the same again. I found the most comfortable position flat on my back and watched Giant cell shower.

He found a brown paper lunch bag and tore off a circular hole. It fit in the sink as a stopper and he filled it with water. Sitting on the toilet and facing the sink he cupped water in his hands and dumped it over his head. A litany of cuss words flew out of his mouth as the pepper spray was reignited. I couldn't help but laugh.

After he was done bathing, the cell floor was a pool of water. He used his T-shirt to mop the entire floor. After he was done he wrung out the shirt in the toilet and went to work polishing the stainless steel sink into a shine. It was my turn to have the cell floor and shower.

This was going to be a long process. We were going to be stuck in the hole for a while. Having been through it once before I paced the length of the cell and explained to Giant what was ahead. Within the next few days we would be getting paperwork. The first set being a lock up order with a 114-D code. It was going to explain we were involved in a riot/melee and deemed security threats. The second set of paper work was going to be reports from prison guards who witnessed the riots. This paper work was listed as a 115 rule violation. Investigators would be coming by cells and to try to get people to talk about the riot. Nobody would say anything, standard issue.

While filling up the sink for a bird bath I studied the building. Above the tray slot on the cell door there was a rectangular piece of Plexiglas to look through. The building was just like all the others on all 4 yards. This was an older style unit. The gun tower was above the vestibule and there was an office for the guards underneath. Underneath the gun tower the wall was painted bright green. There were 3 metal cages spaced along the wall about 10 feet from each other. Each metal cage was about the size of a phone booth. Next to one of the metal cages was a phone. Above the phone in red block letters read: NO WARNING SHOTS. In the middle of the building there was a podium for the prison guards when they weren't in the office. They weren't any where to be seen and were probably involved in escorting other inmates. The two guards in the tower looked busy negotiating which cells the next group of inmates from the riot would fill. I got tired of watching and started my cell shower.

The water didn't seem to help get rid of the pepper spray and it sent a fresh wave of fire on my skin. I stayed on the toilet throwing water on my body for a half hour and finally gave up. After cleaning the cell I looked at the top bunk and Giant was already asleep. His body didn't even fit on the bunk. His feet hung off the edge over the sink.

I got on my bunk and rolled up my shirt into a makeshift pillow. There wasn't a blanket or sheets so I left my pants on and within a minute was out like a light.

Chapter 9 Breaking in the Warden

The Warden sat at the table and looked across at Lieutenant Pickler and asked, "Have you heard anything about any of the other yards going off?

Lieutenant Pickler shook his head no and said, "Not yet. But word of the blood bath is traveling. The other three yards are way to quiet and you know what that means..."

The Lieutenant studied the Warden. It didn't look like he understood the ramifications at all. He helped him figure it out. "It means this prison could be on lock down for years. For the next six months we might have riots on every yard. All the staff will be getting paid time and a half for hazard pay."

The Warden's expression changed with awareness. The Lieutenant smiled a little and realized he was leading the horse to water, time for a little more understanding so he could get the horse to drink. He said, "You know Warden Parker…When we're on lock down it's nice to be able to work extra hours to get paid over time as well as time and a half. Can I work 75 hours this week?"

The Lieutenant watched even more understanding dawn on the Warden's face. It looked like he was mentally doing the math with his own salary as it tripled with the hazard pay and the overtime.

Warden Parker moved some papers around on his desk. He picked one up and studied it. "What are we going to do with the two White inmates involved in the building 23 riot?"

Lieutenant Pickler knew what he was going to do but didn't want to tell the Warden. He said, "You mean inmate Smith and Johnson, who go by the Aka's Giant and B.J… The two with the identity crises?"

The Warden wondered how the Lieutenant knew their names but just said, "Yeah."

The Lieutenant responded, "We do it by the book. They might be sleepers for the Mexican Mafia for all we know. We treat them like southern Mexicans and let the investigation work itself out."

Chapter 10 Post Traumatic Dreams

Though I immediately went into dream land, a deep sleep was elusive. My mind was replaying the riot. It felt like my mind's eye had to know what was happening in every section of the building, like it wasn't enough to remember my parts of the fight. Flashes of the blood stains on the floor dominated with intimate details and each scene would flash back to it. Then, the memory of how the medics had to hold the northern shot caller up while removing his shirt. His eye lids were fluttering and it looked like he just wanted to go to sleep. The medics lifted his arms and somehow I saw him in slow motion and it looked like one of his hands was waving at me.

The rest of my sleep was disturbed by the sounds of the vestibule door clanking open. Iron clanking iron would become an internal alarm clock that would signify shift change at 4 am, but for now was constant. Noises from new inmates that had finally made it into the building arrived. I heard an inmate yell from a cell on the second floor "Hey boy!" There were some other words and it was enough for me to know some of the northerners from our riot had arrived. The inmate recognized someone. I heard Giant wake up and climb down from the bunk and use the toilet. I fell back asleep while he stood at the cell door studying everything and woke back up minutes later to him climbing on his bunk.

For the next couple hours my sleep was like a daydream. It was a cornucopia of violent images from the riot and they flashed by with vivid clarity. It wasn't like a nightmare, more like an outer body learning experience. I knew on some level that this process was a survival mechanism. The immediate lesson of the riot, don't bring your fist to a knife fight. I woke up out of a daze with the knowledge that in a riot with a knife in your hand you don't die. Without a knife in your hand you might.

The morning was off to a slow start. Hunger pains signified that it was way past the usual breakfast time. Both the regular prison guards and the elite guards continued to escort more inmates into cells. We listened to some of the inmates who were housed in the building get ordered by the tower guard to pack up their stuff. They were told where they were going. Some were staying on the same yard and it was only a building transfer. Others were being transferred to one of the other 3 prison yards. It felt like our riot was going to be like a wildfire and surely spread to all of the other yards.

To make matters worse. Prison guards started filling up the building carrying supplies and saying things to incite more tension. I couldn't tell if they were trying to or if they were just naïve. Giant huddled up at the cell door with me to watch.

They were regular prison guards, not the elite unit. We saw brown bedrolls wheeled into the middle of the building by the podium. Other guards had brown plastic cups and spoons. They started putting them in front of every cell and started by us.

An inmate in a nearby cell got a guards attention and asked, "When are we going to get breakfast? We haven't had anything to eat for 36 hours."

The hyped up guard dropped a bedroll and spoke to the inmate. "Probably not anytime soon. This prison has been put on a state of emergency. We aren't even allowed to leave the prison. It's a mess. The news media wants to know what happened."

Another prison guard next to him said, "Building 23 was a blood bath. The northerners got smashed."

Another prison guard said, "Even in their own backyard they got mopped up."

I looked at the cells I knew had northerners in them. The first cell had two bald heads staring at the prison guards. One had a tattoo of a tear drop under his right eye. I saw his eyes cringe and the tear drop lift in anger. Another cell to far away to see as clearly had two big bodies scrunched up against the cell door watching. Every other cell that had northerners had two bodies at the cell door listening. They had to be getting angry and desperate for revenge.

The guards got to our cell and dropped our bedroll. They looked like ex military guys. This shouldn't have shocked them into saying such things in the open. They had to know this wasn't helping calm further riots down. One of the guards took a second look at us and asked, "Are you guys White inmates?"

Giant and I nodded our heads and said, "Yep" in unison.

The guard who asked got the other guards attention and they came to study us. He asked, "What were you guys doing in that riot?"

I said, "Why are you instigating?"

One of the other guards asked, "What building were you guys in?"

We could answer that and both said in unison, "Building 23."

One of the other guards said, "You guys are soldiers to get involved in that!"

A few hours later another set of guards came in with boxes of bag lunches. Other guards carried what looked like blue and red squares of paper sheets. They went to the podium and started writing on each piece. With each piece of paper the guard at the podium communicated with the guard in the gun tower. Both guards would look at a cell like they were making sure of something. It looked like they were going in order and when they got to our cell I realized what they were doing. The blue sheet of paper was going to signify a southern Mexican and the red paper was for the northern Mexicans. The contrast in colors on a big sheet of paper was for the gun tower guard at the control booth and the guards on the floor. It was going to help them not make a mistake and open the cells of rivals at the same time.

The guards started 7 cells down from us and I crammed myself up against the cell door to watch them through a 2 inch space in the side of the cell. A huge metal key was inserted into the tray slot. It folded down and the bedroll and bag lunch went in. Then, the blue sheet of paper was placed on the cell door about 5' feet high. I knew that cell housed a southern Mexican from our building. The same thing happened in the next cell except this time it was a red sheet of paper. I gave Giant the play by play so he knew who was housed in cells nearby.

The prison guards got to our cell. We accepted the bedroll and bag lunch through the tray slot and I saw the blue paper. The guard taped it to our cell and in shock I said, "You guys are making a mistake. We're White inmates."

The prison guard looked at me and then at Giant and said, "So what."

The prison guard was an older White man with brown hair cut in a crew cut. He didn't look like he had any joy in his life or any compassion. His name plate said, Franze. I looked at the other prison guard. He was a

Mexican man, neither had much rank. They were just regular guards. I asked, "What does it say we are on that paper?"

The Mexican guard came over and realized what was happening. He laughed and said, "It says SM, short for southern Mexicans."

I said, "Find a White piece of paper and write WM."

Prison guard Franze gave me an irritated look and said, "What's WM stand for?"

I said, "White Men."

Franze said, "We don't have time for this shit. We're busy."

It was the standard excuse to pass the buck and let someone else deal with the problem. I looked up at the guards in the tower. They were both watching. I tried one last move. "Let me speak to a Sergeant or Lieutenant! You can't label us like this."

Both guards turned away from us and went back to their tasks at another cell. We watched them continue to pass the items through the tray slot. I looked at Giant and said, "They'll fix it when we get to I.C.C."

Giant asked, "What's I.C.C?"

I said, "Inmate Classification Committee. They come by once a week to sort things out. Like deciding who we can go to our 10 hours of yard a week with and other things."

For the rest of the day Giant and I took turns standing at the door. All the other inmates we came in with were starting to make fishing lines to slide out from under their cell doors. The effort was mainly to beat boredom. If someone was lucky enough to have an extra book in their cell it was sought after. One fishing line would slide out of a cell and another fishing line from another cell would cross over it and pull it back in. Then, the book would go sliding into the cell.

I knew that this was our third day in the hole and we were going to have to get into a routine. If we didn't stay mentally busy and positive life would get very depressing.

Chapter 11 Solitary Blues

The next morning I woke up early. Time was starting to slow down and drag by. Being stuck in the cell was becoming claustrophobic. The lack of anything was starting to invade. The proof that other inmates before us had run out of things to do was etched all over the cell in graffiti. A book would have been nice to read. Cards or a chess board would help. We didn't have anything.

Giant woke up with the sound of the breakfast carts. He got down from his bunk and stood at the cell door and asked me some questions.

"When do you think we'll start getting showers and a little yard program?"

I'd been wondering the same thing and had the answer well rehearsed. "We should start getting showers immediately, maybe starting today. They will shower a group of us on one day and the second group on the following day."

Giant nodded his head and said, "That's why they stuck those blue and red sheets of paper on the cells."

I nodded my head and said, "Yup."

I answered the rest of his question. "We won't start getting yard until we get cleared for it at I.C.C. The prison administration has a collection of counselors and staff that will hold court around a table one day a week. That will be a dead day for us without any program or showers. Every other day will have a two hour yard release and showers."

The rest of the afternoon dragged by and showers never came. The only thing that happened was the medical team came. The northerner in our building that didn't die came out of his cell to have his stitches looked at. He was a tall and well built, bald headed Mexican with tattoos covering his body. His neck was blasted in ink with the letters N.S in old English. He sat down at a table while a doctor looked at his neck and side where the stab wounds were. Everything looked okay to the doctor and two prison guards put his handcuffs back on and escorted him back to his cell. He walked with a swagger and I wondered how he could still think so highly of himself after tasting such a lethal defeat. His partner, the shot caller for his crew had died right next to him.

An hour later the building filled up with what looked like plain clothed detectives. Giant huddled up with me at the cell door and we watched them go to a cell a couple doors down. It was an interrogation.

They huddled around the cell and one of the detectives slid some paper work through the side of the cell door. Another detective said, "Inmate Briseno and Alejandro, you are both being charged with being involved in a group melee..."

The detectives went on to explain the level of the state charge and the category it fit in. There were letters to signify the significance of the charge with A) being for anything murder related. B) was a charge that had to do with other heavy offenses related to great bodily injury and pressure moves that had to do with calling shots. C) was a charge that was similar in nature but to a lesser extent. D) was our charge. I knew from being through it that the maximum time they could keep us in the hole on a SHU term was 8 months. Usually it would only be about half of that. Determining factors had to do with prior SHU terms. I explained all of this to Giant.

The next thing the detective said changed the feeling of relief into trepidation.

He said, "We need you to sign this paper. We are sending all of the paperwork related to your case to the District Attorney to see if they want to pick up charges. Since someone was killed there is a good chance some of you will catch additional cases. You have a choice to make. You can waive time on the state charges until the court case either happens or doesn't depending on if the D.A picks it up or you can face the state charges first."

We didn't hear either inmate respond. They had no idea what to do. I worked it out in my mind and decided the best thing to do was waive time on the state charges. If a guilty decision was reached it could be used in court. The court case was by far the worst scenario. Additional years or even a life sentence was a possibility, depending on the priors. For lifers like Johny, this riot was a death blow to any chance of ever getting out.

Everyone in the building heard Johny yell out of his cell. "You have to give them an attorney right now! You can't question them without one! Where's the legal counsel?"

Johny was right. They were already trying to railroad us. If anyone made a mistake and found out they were facing additional charges or a life sentence the courts and the state would be able to use it as leverage. Maybe that was their plan, to find informants.

Both inmates didn't say anything and it was a Mexican stand off. After a few more minutes the detectives seemed to give up. One of them said, "Think about it for a few minutes. We'll come back for your answer."

The detectives came to our cell next. The same thing happened. They slid our paperwork through the side of the cell door and tried the same thing on us. We let them talk without answering. We were studying our paperwork. The first set was the Lock Up Order 114-D and explained why we were in the hole. The second set was the state charge 115 for the riot that was termed a Group Melee.

I scanned through the charges with my mind spinning with worry over outside charges. I found a couple of reports written from prison guards from our building. It didn't look that bad. It only said that I was seen in the area of the fighting inmates punching both fist. It went on to say that pepper spray was administered on me to get me to comply. It didn't say that I was seen running down the stairs.

The detectives were still trying to interrogate us. They were asking all the same questions from the other cell. Johny was still yelling from his cell, "Where's their defense counsel. You can't interrogate them without them knowing their rights!"

I knew the smart thing was to waive time on the state charges but I also felt Johny's stress. If we, the inmates didn't stay somewhat unified things could get ugly. I asked the detective, "What's your name and rank? Who do you work for?"

He responded, "I'm Corrections Officer Lopez and this is my partner Sheldon. We're investigators for the California Department of Corrections."

I said loud enough for the quiet and listening building to hear, "We'll Lopez and Sheldon, I think waiving time on the state charges until the D.A realizes they don't have a case is the smart thing to do. But since I don't see my legal counsel standing next to you to advise me as a lawyer I'm not committing to anything."

I heard Johny yell out of his cell, "That's right!"

Another Mexican yelled out of his cell, "Nobody commit to nothing until we get our legal counsel!"

The detectives tried one more cell next to ours. The two inmates were youngsters at 18 years old and from our building in the riot. One went by the name Pericho and the other went by Sureno. Pericho was a straight gang banger from east LA. You could tell he was just a kid raised by the streets and his mentors were hustlers. Sureno was from the San Fernando Valley and more of an artist. He had drawn up some incredible portraits for both Giant and I.

Both youngsters accepted their paperwork and dutifully listened to the same information and questions. At the end of it they just said, "No comment. We're waiting for our legal counsel to advise us."

A bunch of people in cells yelled their support.

The two detectives looked like they were done trying. They looked up at the tower guard and just stood there. One of the detectives spoke into a microphone quietly and we watched the guard in the tower get on the phone. A couple minutes later we heard the vestibule door opening.

Four prison guards walked into the building. They looked experienced. I focused on the biggest one who seemed to be the one in charge. He was a fifty something year old White man who exuded power. His brown reseeding hair was combed back on a long sloping forehead. He had four red stripes on the right shoulder of his green uniform. He was a Lieutenant.

The detectives who had questioned us walked up to them. They formed a circle and talked for a couple of minutes. Then, one of the detectives pointed to the first cell they tried to interrogate. We were pointed at next. Then it looked like Johny's cell was pointed at.

The building was so quiet you could hear a pin drop. I looked at every cell. A pair of bodies was scrunched up against the cell watching.

I saw the Lieutenant nod his head like he was hearing what he needed to make a plan. He looked up at the prison guard in the tower and spoke into his microphone. Then he walked toward the first cell to refuse the interrogation. The other prison guards and two detectives followed his lead.

The procession looked like a bunch of high school bullies. The two detectives walked with more confidence, like they had their back up. We watched them group up around the cell and the Lieutenant asked in a loud voice, "Why didn't you comply with the investigation?"

Everyone heard the response. "Because we need to know our rights. Aren't we supposed to have legal counsel?"

The Lieutenant asked even more loudly, "Who told you that?"

The inmates behind the cell door didn't say anything, another standoff. The Lieutenant walked to our cell. He stood right in front of the cell and put both his arms up to rest on top of our cell. He asked the same thing.

I read his name off his name plate. I said, "Lieutenant Pickler I'm glad you're here. My cell mate and I are White inmates and we want you to put that on our cell. It doesn't feel right to be labeled another race. Can you help us?"

Lieutenant Pickler gave us an irritated look, like we were messing up his plan with a curve ball. He responded, "I'm not here to talk about that right now. I want to know why the inmates in this building aren't cooperating with my detectives."

I wanted to be a smart ass but knew it wouldn't help. Both Giant and I just stared at Lieutenant Pickler. The angry look on his face seemed plastered there, like it was a mask that didn't change much. His expression seemed to radiate hate.

Without saying a word he walked to the next cell. The two youngsters didn't say a word. The Lieutenant looked like he wasn't used to this. His face got even darker. It felt like he was plotting revenge.

He walked a couple cells down to Johny's cell and the rest of the guards followed him like an entourage. He got right in front of the cell and slammed the palm of his hand against the cell door. The noise reverberated through the building. I felt an immediate burst of adrenaline and anger flood through my body. This was unthinkable.

Lieutenant Pickler put both of his hands on top of the cell door to lean on and looked at Johny. He asked, "Are you an attorney?"

Everyone heard Johny say, "No."

"Then why are you messing up my investigation?"

Johny didn't say anything. He couldn't. Lieutenant Pickler could make his life hell. He could concoct any kind of story he wanted to keep Johny in the hole for the rest of his life. There was too much grey area for him to play with.

Lieutenant Pickler looked like he was at the end of his rope. Then, it looked like he came to a decision. He stepped a few feet away and his loyal procession of guards followed him. He spoke into his microphone quietly to the tower and nodded his head.

The two tower guards walked to the gun rack and one grabbed a block gun and the other one grabbed a 30 mm rifle. The one with the rifle stuck the business end through a port in the bullet proof glass so it was hanging out and facing the ground, but in line with Johny's cell. The other tower guard held his gun at the control booth where he could open Johny's cell.

Lieutenant Pickler walked back to Johny's cell and said, "Do you want to cuff up or do you want to get extracted?"

We didn't hear Johny say anything but it was apparent that he was backing up to get handcuffed. Lieutenant Pickler said, "Smart choice, less painful."

We watched the Lieutenant put the massive key in the tray slot and heard it slam down. The prison guards squeezed in around the Lieutenant protectively like pulling a couple of handcuffed inmates out of the cell was incredibly dangerous.

The tower guard popped the cell open and then ran to the tower window next to his partner. He pointed his block gun directly at Johny as he was backed out of the cell. Lieutenant Pickler made sure all the prison guards had a hand on the two handcuffed inmates and then he walked into Johny's cell.

We couldn't see what he was doing but it became apparent nothing would stay in the cell. A fishing line came flying out to skid down the floor, then a magazine. Then some bed sheets and a couple blankets, then a mattress, then the other one. He was leaving them with only their sheet metal bunks. He came out of the cell and picked up one of the mattresses and ripped it in half and dropped it. He picked up the other mattresses and stuck his hand inside of a torn open section and ripped out some of the stuffing. While he threw the stuffing on the floor he asked, "Am I going to find any contraband in here?"

He threw down the mattress and picked up the fishing line and looked at it. Part of the fishing line was a strip of white bed sheet and the rest of it was a carefully woven line from the threads inside of the boxer shorts along the waistband. The Lieutenant walked over to Johny with the fishing line in his hand and asked, "Is this how you are getting word to all the inmates in this building to lawyer up and mess up my investigation?"

Johny didn't say anything. He just leaned forward with his hands cuffed behind his back looking at the ground.

The Lieutenant continued. "Just remember I can keep you locked up in solitary for the rest of your life! I can get really creative and have been doing this a long time. I can write it up that you're a shot caller and that you are trying to get inmates to kill cops. Do you understand me?"

Johny didn't say anything. He didn't even look up.

The Lieutenant and the rest of the guards circled Johny and his cell mate. They positioned themselves so they all had a hand on an inmate and walked them back to the cell. We watched the cell door close with a resounding thud. Then Lieutenant Pickler stood there with his huge key halfway in the tray slot. He paused and said, "I could just leave you in handcuffs for 24 hours. Maybe that would stop you from interfering with my investigation."

Neither Johny nor his cell mate said anything. A minute went by, then another. Finally the Lieutenant finished putting the key all the way in and the tray slot was slammed open. We saw Johny's wrists stretch out of the cell. The Lieutenant pulled Johny's wrist roughly even further out and we heard Johny grunt in pain as his body bounced into the cell door. We watched his cuffs get released and his hands fly back inside of the cell. His cell mate's wrist came out next and the same thing happened.

One of the detectives smiled like he was enjoying himself now and said something. The prison guards all laughed together and one of them stuck his palm in the air. The detectives all gave each other high fives. The procession of guards followed the Lieutenant back into the middle of the dayroom where they stopped in a circle. The vestibule door cranked and rattled open and they all walked out of the building.

Fifteen minutes later the vestibule door shrieked back open. The same two detectives walked into the building. Two other plain clothed men followed them. The other two men were legal counselors. They explained that the best thing to do was waive the state charges until the District Attorney decided if there was a case to file. They went by every cell and one by one we signed the paper.

Everyone asked questions. "What are the chances the D.A. will make a case out of this?

"It depends on the way the reports are written."

"How much time would the D.A. sentence us too?

"It would depend on the charges."

"How long does the D.A. have to file charges on us?"

"Up to a year but usually within a couple of weeks to a month..."

Chapter 12 The Beginning of a United Revolt

I woke up at 4 am with the sound of the vestibule door rattling open. It was shift change for the guards. The noise of them walking with their keys and gear dangling off their uniforms rang in the quiet building. Then, I heard Johny stop one of the guards as he went by each cell during the head count. He asked as quietly as he could, "Excuse me sir. Can you give us our mattresses back?"

Johny explained what happened. The guard said, "I can't help you right now, maybe later."

I went back to sleep for a couple hours and woke up to the sound of the vestibule door clanging open again. I got up and looked out the cell door. Over 20 prison guards were in a line pushing the food carts through. They were 7 foot high and 4 foot wide stainless steel containers on wheels. While passing out the food through the tray slot I watched a prison guard kick Johny's and his cell mate's mattresses right next to a trash can.

We heard someone side kick the cell door in rapid succession. "Boom!! Boom!! Boom!!"

Everyone knew it was coming from Johny's cell. I felt so bad for him that I yelled a distraction, "When are we going to get showers? It's been 4 days!"

I side kicked my cell door. "Boom!! Boom!! Boom!!"

Other inmates joined in until every cell was kicking their cell doors. It was a good release of pressure.

The prison guards stopped serving the breakfast trays and huddled up in the middle of the dayroom floor. Inmates started yelling.

"When are we going to get yard?"

"You have to let us out of the cell for 10 hours a week!"

After 30 minutes of mayhem the noise died down. The guards started passing out trays again. It felt like everyone was getting frustrated by how vulnerable the situation was. Yesterday we learned we could be kept in this hole for up to a year while the D.A. decided on whether to file charges. We weren't getting showers or yard. It didn't seem like anything positive was going to happen.

A couple of hours after breakfast the detectives came back. They brought more paperwork. More reports about the riot. These reports were from Medical. Every inmate in our building was labeled by name and underneath the name there were two stick figure drawings. In one drawing the figure was facing forward in a standing position with his arms outstretched. In the second drawing the figure was facing the other way in a standing position. Any injuries were noted. I had a cut above my right eye. Giant had a bruise on his right rib area. Other inmates were dotted wherever their injuries were. The extent of the injuries was written as notes off to the side of the drawings. The injuries ranged from bruises or stitches, to concussions, to puncture wounds from weapons, to a dead inmate. The shock came when we got to Johny's paperwork. The only injury on his stick figure that was noted was on the palm of his right hand. Just a little slash on paper but in the note section it elaborated that the wound was consistent with the impact from holding a knife cupped against the palm.

That night my post traumatic dreams were more then vivid. It felt like I could leave my body and see other areas. It started with our building riot. In my mind's eye I was able to see myself running down the stairs so fast that jumping from the halfway spot was the only option to not fall over my feet. I saw myself blocking off a wave of inmates just in time to give Johny enough space to survive and kill. Flinging fists, the sound of shoes screeching on the ground and the noise of war filled my being as if it were happening again. The blood soaked shirts and pools of red stickiness on the floor flashed by with urgency. Then, I was able to see what was happening in the next building. Somehow I saw the riot happening and all the inmates fighting, grunting and going down on the ground. While I was dreaming I wondered if the mental picture was from the information I had found out while in the hole, or if I was able to see it for what it was. While wrestling with the answer in my dream state another question was thrust forward. How did the elite guards show up within minutes? They had to have known the riot was coming just as some of the inmates did. There was no other answer. Lieutenant Pickler's face flashed through my consciousness. Then my dreams went further back, to when I first met Giant on the yard. His short blond hair and chiseled face and good looks were movie star material. I remembered talking to him and finding out he was just like me. A drug addict who was once addicted to the game of selling drugs and the power it brought. I saw images of other inmates who were in prison for the drug game. All of those faces started blending in until I saw the same prison faces fighting in the riot.

Chapter 13 Lets Flood the Building

The next morning the breakfast carts arrived to over 100 angry inmates who were getting closer to exploding in desperation. One inmate started side kicking his cell door, then another followed suit. Soon every cell had an inmate kicking the cell door. The release of energy mixed with adrenaline was like a needed drug to wake up out of a solitary daze. It felt like we were dogs in a cage and instead of barking, we were kicking. "BOOM BOOM BOOM!!"

The prison guards did the worst thing they could do, ignore us.

I knew something was going down. Everyone's collective thoughts and frustrations were gathering momentum and it felt like a toxic energy. I heard a few familiar voices calling out other names and told Giant, "Something is being planned..."

We both stood at our cell door and watched. A southern Mexican inmate on the top tier who we knew had some influence sent out his fishing line. It slid out from under his cell door and lifted off the ground and sailed between the bars and fell to our floor. Then, a line slid out from under Johny's cell and ran over the other one. They both slid under his cell door. A few minutes later Johny called for Pericho to come to his cell door. Then his fishing line flew out across the floor. Eventually our cell was called. We fished in the line and found the note that was going around with a proposition. The note read that we the confined inmates weren't getting our showers or yard. The idea was to flood the building by stopping up our toilets. The desired end result was to get the prison administration to talk to us and speed up the process.

We heard the sound of one toilet after another flushing. Then we heard inmates on the second floor yelling. One inmate started singing, "Here comes the rain again!" The sound of water cascading down in drips was next. Now everyone's toilets were flushing and we heard the sound of water rushing in a torrent and crashing down on the floor with more power. It sounded like it was raining in the building. The water was running under our cell door and I kept trying to push it back with a towel.

Giant got into the adrenaline charged moment and stuffed our toilet with a towel and started flushing. I said, "I guess we might as well flood our own cell. Everyone else's toilet water is filling up our cell anyway.

The vestibule door clanked and shrieked open and an army of prison guards poured into the building. They all had rubber galoshes on their feet and in their hands they held mops and squeegees. We watched them find the right angles to push the water into drainage holes. After seeing our building guards sit on their butts all day while we could have been given showers, it felt good to see them have to work.

One inmate yelled from his cell, "It's about time you earn your paycheck!"

Another prisoner yelled, "About time you get off your asses!"

We watched Lieutenant Pickler walk into the building next. A smaller man with brown hair and glasses was with him in regular clothes. He didn't look like a seasoned prison guard or administrator.

We heard an inmate yell, "That's the Warden! Maybe now we can get showers and yard!"

They talked with a few of the prison guards and came to a decision. Lieutenant Pickler and the Warden branched off. The Lieutenant went up stairs and the Warden walked to the first cell. Giant and I scrunched up against the side of the cell door and watched.

The Warden asked, "What's happening? Why are you guys flooding the cell?"

One of the Mexican inmates inside of the cell said, "Because we aren't getting showers or yard."

The Warden said, "We're working on that. We don't have enough staff yet."

At each cell the Warden assured inmates that the process was moving along. He got to our cell and I threw the kitchen sink at him. "You know Warden that by law under the 8th Amendment of the United States as it intersects with cruel and unusual punishment, the Supreme Court ruled that an inmate must get 3 showers a week and 10 hours outside of the cell in some form of yard."

I studied the Warden as he lifted an eyebrow. He was a decent looking guy who might have some compassion. With brown hair combed to the side in a part and dark brown eyes underneath the glasses on his nose, he looked more like an intellectual than a prison guard. He responded, "We don't have enough staff yet."

I said, "Yeah you do. We watch the building guards sit on their butts all day. It only takes a couple of hours in the morning to run showers for one floor and a couple of hours in the afternoon to run the other floor. You can either get the building guards to handle it or plan on doing at least that many hours of mopping up a flood everyday."

The Warden laughed and studied Giant standing next to me. It looked like he realized we were White inmates for the first time and that reminded me.

I said, "Another thing Warden. We're White inmates. Can you fix it so our cell reflects that?"

It looked like he was strongly considering. He nodded his head and said, "I looked at both of your files and it looks like you don't claim any Mexican gangs and have always been housed as White inmates. Why did you get involved in the riot?"

It was an impossible question to answer and we couldn't so I got philosophical. "California has over 200,000 drug addicts locked up in over 30 California prisons who can't keep up out in the free world. There isn't much rehabilitation in here. Do you think we are all going to sit in a circle and hold hands and sing together? Shit happens."

The Warden said, "I'm going to try to get your showers started tomorrow."

Chapter 14 Who Really Runs the Prison?

The Warden heard the door to his office open. He looked up and saw Lieutenant Pickler. After talking to the inmates yesterday he came to a decision and said, "I want you to help our building guards run showers for the rioters."

The Warden watched the Lieutenant's face react in what looked like disgust. Then he shook his head and said, "Bad idea."

"What do you mean bad idea?"

The Lieutenant leaned down on the table and said, "We don't have authorization for more staff yet from Sacramento."

"So what, we can still let them get their showers. It's almost been a week. They need a shower. Plus, I don't want to have 20 guards in there mopping up the floors all night every night."

The Lieutenant paced back and forth a few times and said, "How do I say this without it offending you sir?"

"Just say it."

The Lieutenant looked right at the Warden and said, "Sir you don't give in to criminals. Those scum bags are the ones who get our kids on drugs. They make our kids think it's cool to get tattoos. Screw their showers."

The Warden responded, "What if they got your kid addicted to drugs and he was in one of those cells. Would you want him to get a shower?"

Chapter 15 Nothing Coming

The next morning I woke up early and stood at the cell door trying to find out if I slept through the 4 am shift change. I looked up at the gun tower. The same two prison guards were still in it.

I heard Giant wake up and looked at him. His blond hair was sticking straight in the air and his eyes had that just woke up confused look. His long body made easy work of climbing down from the top bunk. He lowered a leg to the sink and used his other leg to step down from the bottom bunk to the floor. He realized I was at the cell door and asked, "What time is it?"

I got out of his way and laid down on my bunk so he could use the toilet and said, "I think it's just before 4 am. They still haven't done shift change yet."

While using the toilet Giant asked, "Do you think we'll get showers today?"

I didn't know. It was the question on everyone's mind. After so many days of being stuck in a confined space, one chance to leave for 15 minutes was like the ultimate freedom. More than that, it was proof that time was moving forward and this stay in solitary confinement, however long, was moving forward. I stayed optimistic with my answer, "Yeah, probably today. If not, tomorrow for sure."

Giant nodded his head and stood at the cell door watching the empty building. He looked over his shoulder at me and asked, "Did you have any more of those dreams last night?"

I thought about it and realized this was the first time I couldn't remember my dreams. Maybe my sleep was getting back into a normal rhythm. I answered, "Not that I can remember."

Giant climbed back on his bed and I went back to the cell door. A couple of minutes of staring at the empty building later, the vestibule door rattled and clanked open. Two prison guards came out of the office they were probably sleeping in. They walked out of the building and two other prison guards walked in.

I studied the two Mexican prison guards. They weren't our normal morning guards. Maybe they would have some answers. While watching them get ready to take their first count of the day I looked at all the other cells. Most of the usual suspects were posted at their cell door studying as well. I was getting used to the early bird crew. It was like the inmates in the building were made up of different textures, maybe even different classes or levels. The early birds were usually the veterans and oftentimes the leaders of the cell. They were usually the ones who had done more time. The early birds wanted to know what was coming and prepare for it. In prison the winds of change are subtle.

I looked at Johny in his cell. He was standing at the cell door as usual. He was busy using his fingers for sign language with another inmate in a cell across from me. I found a couple other regulars standing at the cell. We were going to get a feeling for the prognosis for the day. If the Warden was true to his word, he might have already posted a memo for the guards to shower us.

One of the prison guards walked to the top floor and the other one started counting inmates on the bottom floor. While watching from the side of my cell I asked Giant quietly, "Are you awake?"

He made me laugh by saying, "No. I'm still asleep. Why?"

I want to ask the guard if we're getting showers today."

"Go ahead."

The guard had a hard job while we were locked down. All they had to be able to do is count to two, two inmates per cell. When he got to our cell I asked, "Hey boss man. Have you heard if we're getting showers today? Any memos posted?"

The guard said, "Not that I know of."

He kept going. I watched him get to Johny's cell. He asked the same thing and the guard stopped for a minute. The guard kept going and stopped at the cell Johny had been communicating with via sign language. All the early birds were finding out that we still had nothing coming.

After breakfast Giant went back to sleep. I was into a routine where I saved half my breakfast for later. I paced the cell and meditated on thoughts of my upcoming exercise, with periodic stops at the cell door to watch things. The guards didn't look like they had any plans. The two guards in the tower didn't look like anything was happening. It was time to work out.

There was just enough room to do handstand pushups. I stood facing the wall with my back to the toilet and sink and set my hands on the ground about 6 inches from the wall. From there I threw up my feet until my sock filled toes were on the wall. At the end of my reps I tucked my feet back into my body to bring them down in the narrow space. Within 20 seconds I did a set of pushups. Within 20 more seconds I used the toilet for dips. From there I paced the cell for a few minutes until my breathing was controlled and my muscles were ready to get another round.

After lunch it was Giant's turn to workout. We were falling into a natural pattern where he used the cell floor as much as he wanted in the afternoon. Being locked in a cell for 24 straight hours 7 days a week makes every detail about the other person stand out. If a person had bad hygiene, it's amplified. If they snored it was monstrous. If they passed a lot of rotten gas it was noxious. If they had weak conversation and they talked a lot, it was irritating. As each day dragged into another, any and all of the negative qualities were magnified. I was very lucky to have Giant in the cell with me. We were both like kind individuals who were in prison for being out of control drug addicts and dealers. Sober now for the most part, we both held to a certain code of respect and were athletic. We were both good looking, clean and positive thinkers. But the main thing that was going to keep us on the same page, we had total faith in each other to have each other's back when it came to warfare.

While I watched Giant stand at the cell door and lift one knee to his chest and then the other one, I thought about how we were getting along. A few days ago I couldn't take hearing Giant pee into the toilet standing up. After hearing him piss into the toilet over 50 times over the last week, the sound of it was grating on my nerves. Not only had the sound of it hitting the water in a stream bothered me, now I was imagining it bouncing out on the floor or the toilet. Every time he finished using the toilet I couldn't help but look at the floor. A few times, I noticed a few drops on the rim where I sat. I had gotten it off my chest and talked to him about it. He understood my pet peeve and that I was a little bit crazy and gave in. He was now sitting on the toilet to pee like me.

At dinner time everyone was at their cell door watching the guards pass out food. The comments and questions from inmates started right away.

"The Warden said we were going to get showers today!"

"Are you going to run showers after dinner?"

The guards didn't answer. It was obvious they were avoiding a confrontation. They were probably thinking we were going to flood the building again.

Chapter 16 Desperate Times Call for Desperate Measures

The next morning I woke up just before shift change again. Giant woke up and it was a replay of the day before. All the usual suspects were doing all the same things. Watching and communicating with each other. It was the same two Mexican guards and they still hadn't heard about showers for the building.

At 2 pm during the next shift change nothing happened. A few inmates started kicking their cell doors. The frustration was mounting. The awareness that we weren't going to get the promised showers today either, was setting in. I heard a Mexican inmate upstairs yell out of his cell, "Hey Johny! I'm shooting my line!"

Even though I couldn't see the cell on the floor above me, I was beginning to realize who it was. It was that short Mexican who went by Topo who had been in the next building before the riot. I remembered him in my head from the prison yard. He was an older Mexican from east L.A who was a veteran of the California Prison system and an integral part of the gangland scene. At 5'2 and a billboard of ink, he commanded the southern Mexicans like a general, but in a quiet, low key way.

Giant and I huddled against the cell door watching and listening. We heard Topo push something out from under his cell door. It sounded like paper or cardboard. I visualized what he was doing. He was setting up a ramp at an angle to jump his fishing line off of. A couple minutes later we heard his line slide across the floor and saw it lift in the air and flutter down to our floor. Johny whipped his line and we saw it slide under his cell door and onto the floor. The angle was perfect to find Topo's line and it went over it and passed it. Johny gave it a quick yank and his line hooked Topo's and both lines were pulled under his cell.

A few minutes later Johny yelled a name from his cell and we watched him sling his line out. He did the same thing again and again. He was getting word out about another plan. We heard our names called and pulled in his message.

Giant huddled over my shoulder and read the note with me. Greetings brothers: We are going to board up our cells to disrupt the count. We are asking everyone to do this as a show of solidarity. To do this, cover up your cell door with paper or cardboard so the guards can't see inside. As you know, it's been 8 days of our constitutional rights being violated. The Supreme Court ruled a long time ago that 10 hours of yard outside of the cell per week is the minimum to not be considered cruel and unusual punishment. A minimum of 3 showers per week, adequate medical care, laundry and a list of other things that we haven't been getting are also included in a list of demands we'll give the Lieutenant. We flooded the building to get their attention. It didn't work. If we don't keep fighting, we won't get out of the cell any faster.

At the end of the note was a list of boxes with each cell number in it. As it went cell by cell an X was put through the box to establish notification.

Giant looked at me with a confused look on his face and I did some explaining. "Boarding up the cell will keep the guards from being able to count us and they won't be able to call the count in to California's prison headquarters in Sacramento. That will raise the alarms and make paperwork and phone calls happen. We're in a strong position because our rights are being completely violated. It should speed up the process for Sacramento to authorize more prison guards to this building."

Giant said, "They already have enough prison guards in this building."

We watched it daily. The 2 hours of dead time in the morning and afternoon was enough time to escort us to yard and showers.

Every cell had a couple of bodies at the door watching. The first cell to cover their Plexiglas window went dark. Then another cell went dark, and another. All the other cells had light in them. We figured out how to cover the Plexiglas window with some cardboard. The cells that didn't have cardboard used their brown paper lunch bags. It definitely sealed out any view inside. It was hard not to pry open a little crack to look out to see what was happening.

The first prison guard to recognize our plan was in the tower. We heard him call in what he was seeing, "All the inmates are covering their cells to disrupt the count."

We heard a prison guard in the building get off his chair and walk toward us. The tension was building now that the ball was rolling. It was so quiet you could hear a pin drop.

The prison guard said loud enough for everyone to hear, "All you're going to accomplish with this is pain. Are you sure you want us to throw tear gas and pepper spray through your tray slots?"

One of the inmates yelled, "If that's what it takes to get you to start working!"

I kept opening up the window a crack to see what was happening. The hour of the count was upon us and a few other prison guards entered the building. They chatted with the prison guard who had threatened us with pain.

Nothing happened for about an hour. Then, we heard the vestibule door to the building open. Six Inmate Gang Investigators known as I.G.I guards poured in wearing darker green prison guard outfits. They all had insignia stitched on their shoulders and chest that resembled tattoos. They all held large plastic shields in front of them like they were ready for war. The next two that came through had what looked like battering rams. The way they all slowly walked into the middle of the building was a menacing sight. A couple minutes passed.

They knew they were being studied through cracks in the window covers and I realized this was a psychological war. Next, we heard a creaking sound. Through the cracks of our windows we watched the prison guards turn as one toward the vestibule door where the noise was. Slowly, four more I.G.I guards pushed an open cart that was filled with gear 8 feet high. It was an imposing sight of riot gear. More shields and battering rams were stationed pointing in the air. Also on the cart were cardboard boxes with red lettering that said, TEAR GAS. I watched one of the guards stick his hand inside another cardboard box. He pulled out pepper spray canisters the size of fire extinguishers and passed them out.

For half an hour nothing happened. The prison guards just stood there. I remembered my first trip to the hole in solitary when we boarded up our cells. The extraction by the guards was a painful process. To make it less painful we had taken our thin mattresses off our bunks and wrapped ourselves in them. Wrapped up inside the mattresses like a hot dog in a bun, we leaned against the cell door as the extraction team mounted up just outside it. Eventually the guards always made it in the cell spraying pepper spray and tear gas. The mattresses were our buffer against the noxious gases. I explained all of this to Giant and we started practicing our positions.

Giant was 4 inches taller then me and weighed about 30 lbs. more then my 200 lbs. He was going to be our rear. That meant I was going to be the one scrunched into the cell door with Giant behind me pushing as hard as he could. It was both of us against one battering ram. I practiced lowering my body like a football player who was a lead blocker. I had to keep all of my weight on the tray slot. Giant lowered himself against me like another blocker to pin me against the tray slot even tighter. They weren't going to get through us.

We took turns studying the prison guards. While Giant was watching through the crack he counted them out loud. "There are 18 of them so far."

I asked, "How big are the guards holding the battering ram?"

"As big as me or bigger."

I asked, "Are they going to be able to break through us?"

"Nope."

It sounded by his tone that he was losing confidence. I took a turn looking out the crack in our window and another army of prison guards poured in like a tsunami. They looked like they were on steroids and meth. They looked like they meant business. They looked like criminals. I told Giant, "Things are heating up. It looks like the veterans just arrived."

I looked at some of the other cells in the building. Everyone was reacting to the awareness that the level of this fight had just escalated. Instead of one inmate barely looking out through a crack in the window both inmates were scrunched into that ever widening crack. A few cells took the window cover completely off and were immediately yelled at by other inmates and put it back on. Fear was creeping in. What felt like total control and a victory for us, was now feeling like a hopeless, desperate, un-winnable war?

Giant stated what every inmate was thinking. "We're screwed. The prison guards are going to be able to smash us up and say we assaulted them to get away with whatever they want. Once they get in a cell, they can shut the door where nobody can see anything and then handcuff us to the toilet or bunk and stomp us out with their boots or with that battering ram."

I knew he was right but I didn't want that kind of thinking to dominate us into a fearful paralysis. It already was. What we needed was more positive thoughts. While looking out the window I said, "This is all for show. They don't want to do this any more then we do. But if they do, remember how freaking strong we are. We train our body's way harder then they do. Plus, mentally we have been to hell and back. This is a walk in the park for us."

We watched for another agonizing and slow moving hour before something happened. A Lieutenant entered the building. It wasn't Lieutenant Pickler, but he was also a monster of a white man at 6'4 and over 240 lbs. He stood next to the most dominant looking I.G.I. guard.

The I.G.I. guard was of Mexican descent and he looked pretty seasoned. He looked like he enjoyed this kind of stuff. He talked to the Lieutenant and I read his lips say, "We start with the bottom tier."

The Warden and Lieutenant Pickler walked into the building. We all watched Lieutenant Picker huddle up with the other Lieutenant and the I.G.I guard. You could tell he knew them well. I began to realize this was his prison, not the Wardens.

An inmate yelled out of his cell. "Hey Warden! You said we were getting showers! What happened?"

The Warden looked in the direction of the yelling inmate and wasn't able to find him with all the windows completely or partially covered. It made him look like he was out of his element and uncomfortable with the situation. He looked at Lieutenant Pickler taking over with the I.G.I. team. Then he turned and walked out of the building through the vestibule.

Lieutenant Pickler was completely taking over the operation. He pointed right at our cell. It didn't make sense. We weren't the last cell in the corner of the building. We were 6 cells down from it. They were picking on us because we were the only White inmates involved in the riot. Maybe they thought we were softer and could be made an example of. Maybe they had a plan to make us look bad or set us against the Mexican inmates.

Lieutenant Pickler took a step back. He was taking a back seat and it looked like he wasn't going to get his hands dirty with the cell extraction process. We watched the lead I.G.I. guard huddle with a few of his members. Again, they looked right at our cell and pointed at us. He spoke to them with his hand covering his mouth and then they broke apart. Their plan was in motion.

A couple of the I.G.I guards got behind the cart and pushed it at an angle that was headed right to our cell. The other I.G.I guards walked next to it and pulled items out. The biggest guard pulled out the battering ram. They got to about 10 feet from our cell and stopped and stared at us. Giant and I couldn't help staring at them from two different cracks in the cell window.

The Lieutenant walked past the imposing cart of gear and I.G.I guards and came right to our cell. I felt my anger rising that we were being picked on. Why were they? What was their strategy?

Just as the Lieutenant got to our cell we closed the cardboard up tight and blocked off our cell door. We stuffed our mattresses in front of us for protection in case they tried to get in.

Instead, the Lieutenant tapped the large metal key against the metal cell door and the noise echoed loudly throughout the entire building. The silence after was palpable. We were on the stage.

I answered with, "Is it finally shower time or yard release?"

My mind was spinning with thoughts like a tornado about what to say? I didn't want to take the role of mouthpiece for our struggle. We were two White inmates involved in a riot with over 100 Mexicans fighting against each other. It wasn't our job or position and the pride of the Mexicans would definitely fight against it. It was a set up.

The Lieutenant said loudly, "We want to talk this out with you so nobody gets hurt. This doesn't have to happen."

We didn't say anything. I pushed against Giant to let him know to move. He gave me enough space and I turned and put my mattress against my back to lean on against the cell door. I told him what I was thinking. A few minutes passed.

The Lieutenant rapped his keys against our cell door again and the noise was excruciating. The echo reverberated throughout the silent building and my anger nearly erupted. I yelled out, "We aren't letting you decide who our spokesman is! We are just one of many in this building who hasn't had a shower or yard in almost 9 days!"

Another inmate yelled from inside his cell, "That's right! We want our showers and yard!"

The Lieutenant yelled, "This isn't how you get us to do you any favors!"

We resumed our positions against the cell door. I had my mattress wrapped around my face and upper body and lowered myself so my forearms were squeezing it against the tray slot. Giant positioned himself behind me and I felt his mattress against my back. We heard the Lieutenant say quietly to his extraction team, "Let's get this started."

We couldn't see anything. But we heard the key go into the tray slot. The sound of it dropping open outside of the cell was replaced by feeling a steel bar jabbed into my forearms. I strained against it and held. Whoever was holding it on the other side pulled it back out and slammed it back into me. It was pushing my mattress all over the place. Giant was pushing against me so hard that it moved the mattress even further. It almost slipped all the way off just as the steel battering ram was pulled back out for another thrust. In desperation a better idea hit me. Instead of using the mattress as a wrapper around my upper body and face, I left it off me. It was already scrunched up in the space of the tray slot so I folded it against it even tighter and stuffed my body against it. Giant squeezed against me just as I felt the battering ram slam into us. They were blocked. I felt the guard with the battering ram give up and listened.

Through the adrenaline filled haze, the sound of inmates were kicking their cell doors and their yelling invaded my consciousness.

"Hell yeah!"

"Come and get us coppers!"

"Keep on knocking! Nobody's home!"

"Screw your head count!"

"Give us our showers and yard!"

I heard one of the prison guards on the other side of the cell door say something in his microphone that changed things.

"Have the tower pop their cell door open while I'm ramming."

They were going to pop our cell door open on the rollers so it opened from the side at the same time. That meant we had to hold our position against the tray slot and try to hold the door closed. They were going to have at least 3 guards pushing the cell door open at the same time. We heard one of the guards speak into his microphone.

"Pop cell 7!"

A few seconds later we heard our cell door click. The cell door jerked hard and opened a few inches. I stopped pushing against the tray slot and tried to hold the door. It was opening further and hands were getting inside. As the guards grabbed the cell door in a grip they overpowered us. The door opened halfway and a torrent of pepper spray drenched me. The impact against my face caused me to jerk backward into Giant who lost his balance. He fell forward and I landed on my butt. I heard the prison guards screaming orders.

"Get down! Get down!"

I felt Giant fall down on top of me and could feel the guards inside of our cell grabbing me. I was in no man's land. If I resisted the guards would be able to give me more charges and beat the hell out of me. I felt hands grab my ankles and I was yanked out of the cell. More hands grabbed me and turned me so I was face down. I felt my hands yanked behind my back and handcuffs secured around my wrist.

I looked at Giant. Three guards were standing over him inside of the cell. He was lying on the floor on his back with his fist in front of his face to ward off any attack. I saw his white boxer shorts and stomach plastered with orange pepper spray. The guards were yelling orders.

"Turn over! Get on your stomach!"

One of the guards stomped his boot into Giant's midsection and I realized why he had his fist in front of his face. With Giant still in the cell the guards had free reign to get more violent without witnesses. Giant's forearms held on to the guards ankles the second time. He was trying to keep the guard from being able to lift his leg. The guard responded by hammering his boot rapid fire. I saw Giant's chest getting pummeled and yelled, "Stop kicking my cellie!"

My yell pierced the entire building and time seemed to slow down. I saw two of the guards in the cell turn and look at me. Another guard inside the cell grabbed Giant's ankles and yanked him skidding on his back out of the cell. The guards roughly flipped him on his stomach and yanked his arms behind his back and cuffed him.

The noise of the building hit me in waves that got louder. Everyone was kicking their cell door and yelling profanities. The energy felt like it was on the verge of exploding and time seemed to speed back up.

I felt two prison guards grab me under my arms and lift me to my feet. My body was surrounded by guards who all had a hand on me. They pushed me toward a metal cage and one said, "We're putting you in the phone booth for a while."

A couple of prison guards ran ahead. They opened the metal cage and I was slammed inside. There was barely room to turn around and I bounced off the metal walls with my shoulders and saw the door slam inches in front of my face. The cage had holes in it that looked like honey comb. I could see through it but at a distance it was hard to focus. I squeezed closer and rested my head against the door and chose two holes to look through.

Giant was being lifted to his feet by his arms handcuffed behind his back. It forced him to lean over at an angle. He shook his face as if he was trying to avoid the agony of the pepper spray. There was an orange streak on his chin running down his chest. His white boxer shorts were drenched. The prison guards escorted him to the cage next to me.

Giant didn't fit in the cage standing up straight. He had to bend at the waist and stand in a crouch. He found the most comfortable position and leaned his head against the metal door like I was.

I studied the building from this side. All the cells had their windows blocked and it was an eerie feeling. It reminded me of when I was a kid and I thought that if I shut my eyes or put my hands in front of them nobody could see me. It didn't work then and it wasn't working now.

Lieutenant Pickler walked toward our cages with a smug look on his face. He stood as tall as he could and tilted his head back while studying Giant crouched in his cage. He pretended to look like he cared and said, "Boy that looks like it hurts! They sure drenched you with pepper spray."

Giant grunted in pain and didn't even look at him. He rested his head against the cage and he took a raggedy breath of air. His chest heaved like he was having trouble breathing.

Lieutenant Pickler walked a few paces and stared at me. Unlike Giant I gave him a look. He asked me, "Who called this shot? Who told you to board up your cells and disrupt my count?"

I stopped looking at him. Instead, I looked at Giant. He didn't look like he was getting enough air. He began wheezing.

I yelled at Lieutenant Pickler, "Get him in the shower before he dies!"

I glanced at the Lieutenant. His face darkened into an evil grimace. Then, he kicked right at me and his boot slammed into the cage I was in.

"Hey punk, you don't tell me what to do! Your friend can die for all I care."

The lead I.G.I. guard turned toward us and yelled, "Pickler! We're going in the next cell!"

Pickler put his thumb in the air and nodded his assent. I watched the extraction team mount up. They surrounded the cell. The guard with the battering ram lined it up with the tray slot. Another guard put the key in the slot, turned it and yanked the tray slot open. The Mexicans in the cell had a mattress already stuffed against it. The battering ram was kept at bay. The guard holding it brought it back and lowered his body to slam it in again. This time the mattress moved a little and an opening appeared. An I.G.I guard standing on his right tried to stuff a tear gas grenade inside but the hole closed back up with the mattress. Three guards to the left of the guard with the battering ram grabbed the side of the cell door. The cell door popped and was yanked sideways. The Mexican inmates weren't ready for it. The first inmate lost his mattress in front of him and his tattooed down body in white boxer shorts filled up the space. The guards fanned out and sent streams of pepper spray into the cell. The inmate's faces looked bewildered as the guards rushed into the cell. The first inmate fell to the ground. He was lying on his back with his eyes partially closed to avoid the pepper spray. I watched the first guard to get in the cell stomp his boot down on the crumpled and partially blind inmate's chest. He stomped his boot again and again. The other Mexican in the cell still stood in a crouch and had his mattress somewhat wrapped around him. He ran at the guard stomping on his cellie and bulldozed the stomping guard backward. That guard fell backward off balance into another guard.

The building erupted into a frenzy of noise. There was a constant and repetitive slamming of plastic cups against metal cell doors in almost every cell. It sounded like a hundred echoes per second. A number of cells had inmates side kicking the cell door to add a deeper, louder boom in the echo chamber. On top of that inmates were screaming obscenities.

"Kick that cop's ass!"

The I.G.I team swarmed around the two inmates. Four guards grabbed the first inmate and turned him over. His hands were lifted behind his back by one guard, while another guard stepped on the inmate's back and another guard kneeled on the back of the inmate's legs to hold him to the ground in a pinch.

The same thing happened with the other inmate and they were both lifted to their feet. One inmate was brought to the third metal cage on our side. The other inmate was escorted to the other side of the dayroom for an empty cage.

The noise in the building died down to a lesser roar. Everyone wanted to watch. Cracks appeared in cell windows. Faces filled up the window spaces. Watching the guards storm the cell was intoxicating entertainment.

Everyone heard the vestibule door as it shrieked and clamored open. The Warden walked into the building like he was on a mission. He looked right at Lieutenant Pickler and said, "Come here."

The two prison administrators talked and I couldn't hear what they were saying. The building got even quieter. Lieutenant Pickler shook his head in disgust and I heard his voice get louder. The Warden didn't waver and kept a resolute posture. He stepped back and spoke into a microphone to the tower guard above him.

I looked at the guard in the tower and for the first time realized there were guards everywhere. At every porthole every few feet a guard had a gun pointed. Rifles hung out the window a few feet facing the floor. The gun tower guard standing at the control podium listened to the Warden give him an order. He positioned himself in front of the microphone and tapped on it. It sent a noise we were familiar with through the speakers. It meant an announcement was on the way.

"ATTENTION IN THE BUILDING. THE WARDEN WANTS YOU TO KNOW HE JUST GOT OFF THE PHONE WITH SACRAMENTO. YOU WILL BE RECEIVING SHOWERS IN THE MORNING. YOU WILL ALSO BE SEEING I.C.C TO GET YARD."

The building erupted in cheers. One by one the inmates removed the window covering. Soon all the inmates were visible standing at their cell doors watching.

One inmate yelled, "It's about time!"

Chapter 17 Taking Back the Prison

The Warden held the phone to his ear and said, "I did what you told me and it worked. The inmates stopped obstructing the count and took down their window covers."

Prison Administrator Jones from the California Department of Correction's headquarters in Sacramento thought about the earlier conversation with the Warden. His voice was strained and it was obvious he was in over his head. Being a new transfer it was understandable he was fighting against the established hierarchy. Jones said, "Warden Parker you have to continue to establish yourself like you did tonight. It's your prison. Everyone underneath of you will respect you for doing so."

The Warden thought about Lieutenant Pickler. He was right about one thing. We need an authorization for more staff, or more overtime to run the building right. He asked, "How long until the paperwork is processed to get more staff?"

Jones said, "Probably another week. Just do what you can with what you have until then. As long as the inmates see things starting they'll calm down."

The Warden hung up the phone right when Lieutenant Pickler stormed in.

The Lieutenant yelled, "What are you doing? A lot of the staff here lost a lot of respect for you tonight!"

Warden Pickler stood up from his desk and said calmly, "This is my prison Pickler. I am going to run it, not you."

The Lieutenant tilted his head back and scowled. Then he said, "You need the help of all the integral components who know this prison better then you. If you don't have us, you don't have this prison."

Chapter 18 Shower Time Wino

I woke up to the vestibule door grinding open at 4 am. The pepper spray was still burning on my skin. It felt like my neck was turning into rubber. I stood at the cell door and watched the two Mexican guards enter. A few minutes later they split up and did the head count. At our cell I nodded my head and the guard jumped back in surprise. Every other inmate must have been on their bunk sleeping until me. I looked at his name plate, Hernandez. I laughed quietly and squeezed myself tight against the side of my cell door and asked quietly, "Are we getting showers today?"

Hernandez nodded his head and said, "I think so. That's what we're hearing."

I turned and saw I woke up the Giant. He was sitting on his bunk staring at me through tired eyes with his blond hair sticking in the air like a porcupine. He asked, "What's the word?"

"It sounds like we're getting showers today."

Giant climbed down from his bunk to use the toilet and I got out of his way. Just knowing we were going to get showers today had me feeling optimistic. The gloom and doom of solitary confinement with nothing on the horizon was so depressing, it was oppressive.

Giant said, "I hope we get I.C.C too."

I was way ahead of him in my excitement. As soon as we were cleared by the committee we were going to be able to get store once a month. We were hungry. I told Giant, "Once we get cleared by I.C.C our time in solitary will start to fly by."

After breakfast almost every inmate stood at the cell door watching for a sign of showers. Nothing happened. The building was completely empty. Maybe the guards were all meeting and briefing about how to handle it.

An hour later the vestibule door shrieked and rattled open. Nobody walked into the building. That meant whoever entered was walking up the stairs to the gun tower. The Warden's head popped up. He was by himself. He talked with the two guards and they walked to the window that looked out at the yard.

Giant said, "He's waiting on more prison guards."

An hour passed and the Warden walked into the building with the two building guards. We heard the Warden ask, "Where's the rest of my staff?"

One of the guards said, "I guess they're all busy..."

The Warden shook his head and walked to the first cell on the bottom floor. I scrunched up close to the cell door to look out the side and watch.

The tower guard tapped on the microphone to warn us of an announcement and said, "Attention in the building! Shower time! You have 10 minutes to shower."

The building erupted in jubilation. Inmates yelled and kicked their doors. A number of the inmates seemed addicted to banging their cups against the metal cell door what seemed like million times an hour. One inmate yelled for the Warden to come to his cell. We heard him ask all the questions we were wondering.

"Are you going to run I.C.C. today?"

"Are we going to be able to order store food? We're starving and we don't have any cosmetics for hygiene!"

The Warden answered that he was going to run I.C.C this afternoon and that we would be able to order from the store after that.

The Warden ran the two southern Mexican inmates through the drill and handcuffed them. The tower guard at the control booth popped the cell and one inmate walked out backward and then the other. The Warden walked in between both inmates with a hand on each one. The other two guards held the outside edge and held the shoulder of a prisoner. Both southern Mexicans looked disoriented from being in a cramped space for 10 days. They only had white boxer shorts and a towel. Both were in their early twenties. I studied their tattoos to see where they were from. Both had LA neighborhoods plastered on their bodies in ink. One was from Norwalk and had AVENUES blasted across his stomach. The other one had LA blasted on the back of his bald head. Underneath it on the back of his neck it said, 18th Street. They passed our cell and stopped at the first set of showers on our floor. The Warden turned his key in the steel shower door and pulled it open. The two inmates walked in. The inmates took turns backing up and sticking their wrists through the tray slot to get the handcuffs removed. One of the guards handed them some soap and a razor.

The Warden and two building guards walked by our cell to get two more inmates. We watched the same thing happen. The two inmates backed out of the cell in only boxer shorts holding a towel. Both northern Mexicans were in their 30's and I remembered seeing them on the yard and tried to place which building they had lived in. Instead of walking like normal people, they both dragged their left leg in a swagger. As they walked by I was tempted to ask them if they blew out a tire. They passed and one of them had hair all over his back. The other one had a big SF in block letters on his back to represent that he was from San Francisco. They swagger stepped to the middle showers.

When our turn came I looked at the Warden and said, "Thanks for getting this started."

He smiled and nodded his head. "Your welcome. Let me do a quick search. Lift up your hands... Open your mouth... Lift up your testicles... Turn around... Lift up each foot... Spread apart your ass cheeks... Squat and cough three times..."

After we followed the strip search procedure, I backed up to the cell door and stuck my wrist through. Then Giant did the same thing. We walked the length of the building to the far showers. It felt like a trip to Disneyland to get out of the cell after a week and a half. It was disorienting. Every cell had inmates stuffed up against it. A number of inmates who knew us yelled our names.

"Hey B.J! Thanks for coming to the hole with us!"

"Giant what's up you big baller?"

We didn't know which cells to look for. Mexican bald heads were at every door. Over seventy percent of the inmates were northern Mexicans and I found myself nodding to some of them as if they were southern Mexicans I might know.

At the shower door the Warden put the key in. The shower door was a massive steel barrier that looked like it weighed over 200 pounds. It creaked open and we both stepped in. It shut with a resounding clank. We got our handcuffs off through the tray slot and accepted soap and a razor from one of the building guards. He said, "I'll be back for the razor in fifteen minutes."

The shower had three shower heads and it felt incredible to feel the water rushing all over my body. I lathered up my hair and face. Standing under the water naked felt so good I didn't want to move. As I lathered up my face and neck I realized how much my facial hair had grown. On the shower wall there was a stainless steel mirror. I looked at myself. Wild blue eyes stared back at me. I noticed Giant was staring at himself in the mirror and I heard him grunt.

I laughed and said, "I look like an animal!"

Giant cocked his neck at different angles to study his reflection further and said, "I look like a circus freak."

I laughed way too hard. My laugh made Giant start laughing out of control but he was still cocking his head in different directions and studying himself in the mirror. That made me laugh even harder. I was starting to understand that being confined to a cell like a dog in a cage brings about insanity.

I picked up my tiny razor and said to Giant, "The zoo animals don't get a complete razor."

That caused another gleeful eruption of laughter out of both of us. We weren't ready to go to any social gatherings.

Trying to use the mini razor forced me to concentrate. It was nearly impossible to hold the one inch long razor and control it. I scraped the safety razor all over my face. My facial hair wasn't coming off. It took the entire fifteen minute shower to shave somewhat well. With the Warden and guards standing at the shower door I quickly lathered up my body for a final cleansing.

On the way back to our cell I tried to figure out who the different inmates were and realized all I had to do was look at the red or blue sheet of paper stuck to the cell door. The color contrast not only made it easier for the prison guards to know who the enemies were, it made it easier for us. I knew that as the building evolved, the inmates with the most influence would come to the surface. It was going to take listening and watching. We made it back to our cell. Our 15 minutes of freedom was over.

The Warden was true to his word. In the afternoon a group of prison administrators walked into the building. I counted eight people. All but two of them were in plain clothes. The two in uniforms looked like a Sergeant and a Lieutenant. The Warden ushered them all into the office underneath of the gun tower.

I looked at the guard in the tower. He tapped on the microphone and sent the audible sound through the speakers. He announced, "Listen for your name for the I.C.C hearing."

A noise explosion filled the building. I found myself screaming in joy. Everyone was releasing pent of frustration with yells of jubilation that this part of hell was almost over. The tower guard tapped on the microphone again and everyone got quiet in anticipation.

"Inmate Briseno! Get ready for I.C.C"

A couple of minutes later the building guards walked to Briseno's cell and brought a jumpsuit for him to wear. He was strip searched and then he backed out of cell wearing his new clothes. We watched him walk into the office. Ten minutes later he came out of the office and was hit with a barrage of questions.

"When did they say you get yard?"

"How about store?"

Briseno answered, "No yard for at least a week. I get to order store next draw.

Giant and I watched inmates go to their I.C.C hearings for the rest of the day. We found out that our yard was still being delayed by a lack of staff. We also found out that eventually we would get some of our property related to what we owned that was on the solitary store list.

Chapter 19 New Arrivals and New Problems

For the next week we watched the program begin to start. We were only getting a shower every third day but they were running I.C.C every day. The oppressive atmosphere was slowly lifting as we headed into our third week in solitary.

Every time the guard in the gun tower tapped the microphone we were hoping our name would get called. Instead, we watched all the other inmates as a form of television. At shower time we studied all the northern Mexicans. Almost all of them were blasted banners of tattoo ink. Most of it was related to cities. Most of the cities were cut short into abbreviations. San Jose was cut to San Jo. Modesto, Stockton, San Francisco, Sacramento, Monterey, Watsonville, Gilroy and other cities were abbreviated on inmate's backs, stomachs, necks and on the back of bald heads. The harder core gang members either had NS or NF on their chests or for the even bolder, their necks or foreheads.

The southerners were a different breed. They were all about Mexican pride combined with the culture of southern California. The southern Mexicans were Chicanos. Big cities like LA, with all the stardom and glamour made it a gangster's paradise. It was reflected in their looks. They were gangster stars of the street. Opulent Orange County inspired a lot of gangs in Santa Ana, Orange, Westminster and Anaheim. These guys looked like they were soldiers willing to do whatever was expected. San Diego, being close to the border had a lot of drug trafficking gangsters. These gangsters had a cartel look. The Inland Empire with cities like San Bernardino, Riverside, Yucca Valley, Palm Springs, Lake Elsinore and the Valley's of desert that stretched to the border of Mexico had a lot of gangster's close to the cartels and plenty of places to bury bodies. These gangsters looked like they had seen it all and were comfortable with it. For the most part, the southerners had two distinct styles. The older ones either had a low rider style or an Aztec warrior style. They were at odds with the northerners mainly because they didn't have

Mexican pride. Many of the northerners acted like they wanted to be Black folks.

My dreams were much less vivid and I was having a hard time remembering them clearly. In the ones I could recall, I remembered our relationship with Johny on the yard before the riot. He always remembered our birthdays and somehow put together presents for us. I remembered specific times he would show up at my cell early in the morning before breakfast with a smile and greeting, like he was glad to see me. The dream study of Johny seemed to be about how to judge him. I began to see him as a good leader for his people, like a mother hen in charge of her flock. It was obvious he cared about the youngsters under him and he shepherded them with a protective love. He didn't fit into the low rider style or the Aztec warrior style. He was just a human, stuck in prison for life over some bad decisions as a kid, who was surviving prison with honor and dignity. The rest of my dreams that I could remember seemed to be about wrestling with why I had gotten involved in the riot. Was it loyalty to friends, or was it just pure pride?

A few of the inmates in our building got transferred to the regular solitary Administrative Segregation building next door. This opened up room in our building for the mainline population inmates already getting full program on the yard to trickle back in. One of the new occupants was a southern Mexican. He moved into a cell above us but over one cell.

The cells have a vent over the toilet that is connected to the cell next door and the two cells above. Our neighbors in the cell next to us were southerners. The names they went by were Shadow and Danger. We listened to their conversations.

"Hey brothers who's on the yard from east LA? Can you tell them we're over here and get us a care package?"

That afternoon the two new mainliners came back from yard with a laundry bag full of goodies for our neighbors. They walked through the vestibule straight to their cell next to us. The two guards in the tower got the two guards attention on the floor. Then, one of the guards in the tower tapped on his microphone and spoke into it.

"Bring that bag to the podium."

One of the guards walked from the podium halfway to meet the inmate. After a couple minutes of discussion the guards sent the inmates directly back to their cell.

As soon as we heard the upstairs cell slam shut, we heard one of our neighbors climb on the toilet and start a conversation.

"Thanks for trying to get us all of that food! Tell the guys on the yard we said thank you!"

The southern Mexican upstairs said, "There's still a way for us to get you most of this stuff."

"How?"

By wrapping it all up in plastic wrap until its water proofed. Then we can flush it from our toilet to your toilet."

"How?"

"If we both flush our fishing lines at the same time they will both wrap around each other. Then we pull your fishing line into our cell and tie your water sealed package to it. Then you pull it until it enters through your toilet."

They both flushed their line down the toilet but held on to the end of it. The lines spun around each other and became one knotted line. Fishing was getting a whole new meaning. With enough plastic wrap to seal the packages, our neighbor's were able to pull goods from cell to cell through the toilet.

The upstairs mainline inmates became a conduit for all of the southern Mexicans in solitary in our building. They were getting the most sought after store good, coffee, and breaking it into portions to share with everyone.

The next two mainline prisoners to move in our building landed right above our cell and they were White inmates. I stood on the toilet to talk into the vent and got their attention.

"Excuse me! Cell 207!"

Both Giant and I heard the two inmates come to the vent. One responded, "Yeah? What's up?"

I introduced us.

"Hey brother are you guys White inmates?"

"Yeah! I'm Dirty Dan from Sacramento and my cellie is John from Modesto!"

We attempted the same thing our neighbor's had. We found out that I only had one homeboy on the yard from my county. Giant had a lot more from San Francisco.

The next morning both of us stood at the cell door to watch our new mainliners go to yard. The two White inmates looked like veterans of the prison system. One had a tattoo on his forehead for some reason and I saw his brow and tattoo crease while he walked to the vestibule and studied our cell at the same time. We thought he was trying to see what we looked like. The two inmates disappeared into the vestibule and I realized what he was studying. He was confused over the blue sticker on the door signifying we were southern Mexicans.

A couple of hours later when the morning yard was called back in, we watched our new connections walk back in. Dirty Dan led the way with his cell mate behind him. As he got to the stairs about 25 feet away he used his right hand to tell us to talk through the vent. I watched him climb the stairs and read his tattoo on his forehead. It said SAC in block letters, short for Sacramento.

He went straight to the vent.

"Hey B.J! I thought you said you were White inmates. Are you trying to get over on us?"

I couldn't help but laugh. Giant responded behind me, "We're White!"

I heard Dirty Dan and John talking. John reminded Dirty Dan that they heard there were 2 White inmates involved in the big riot on the other yard.

Dirty Dan asked, "Are you the 2 White inmates who got involved in that big riot?"

Relieved that they understood I said, "Yep. That's us."

"Oh, alright, sorry for doubting you but did you know your cell says you're southern Mexicans?"

I said, "Yeah we know. We've been trying to get them to fix it."

Dirty Dan said in all seriousness, "You guys need to fix that. It could cause you some major problems."

I didn't like the words he used. In prison you don't tell another man that he needs to do anything unless you're ready for the consequences. I didn't say anything and the lack of conversation said it all. There was a thick element of tension setting in. This conversation was the kind you don't have through a vent or in front of other people. I knew our southern Mexican neighbors were listening, as were the inmates above them.

Dirty Dan asked, "Did you hear me?"

I felt my anger rising but held my mouth shut. I wanted to tell him it wasn't his business to tell me what I needed to do. But all that would have done was force my hand. Giant didn't hold his temper as well and he paced the cell saying, "Dude needs to stay out of our business before he gets himself in a wreck."

I knew all 3 cells connected to our vent heard Giant. I spoke up, "Dirty Dan we know how to do prison time."

He responded, "I didn't mean to make you have a bad day. I just wanted to tell you what the White inmates are saying on the yard. One other thing they will wonder about when they hear about this is why did you get involved in the riot?"

Now I was ready for war again. Being questioned wasn't what I had in mind. Instead of getting a little love from our White race in the form of something to eat and some coffee, we were being ganged up on. I said, "This is the kind of conversation you have on paper, not on the airwaves."

I heard our neighbor's agree by saying the equivalent to, that's right, in Spanish.

I realized how to deal with it. I had to put the problem in their face and question them. "Hey Dan do the White inmates have a side of the dayroom in each building?"

Dirty Dan said, "Yeah."

I continued, "Are the northern Mexicans and Black inmates allowed to walk or run into your dayroom?"

"No that isn't allowed, we aren't allowed to go through their side of the dayroom either."

I turned the interrogation on them. "So if the northerners or Black inmates ran into your side of the dayroom you wouldn't do anything about it?"

Dirty Dan said, "We wouldn't allow that either. Is that what happened in your riot?"

I said, "That's what happened in our building and we had the southern Mexican's back."

Chapter 19 The Problem Gets Bigger

Dirty Dan said he didn't mean to ruin our day. But that's exactly what he did. That's all we thought about. I took turns with Giant pacing the cell floor discussing the issue and our future.

While I walked the length of the 10 foot long cell I problem solved the situation. "Let's look at it from the perspective of the White race on this yard. They are probably looking at it like we could end up on this yard after we finish our solitary confinement time. Imagine if we don't get this straight in time. What if the prison administration decided to label us southern Mexican inmates and housed us in a southern Mexican cell. That would be a huge problem."

Giant began to see the problem more clearly. He said, "So what do we do if they don't fix it at I.C.C. and it actually happens?"

I thought about it. The southern Mexicans wouldn't want it to happen either. To be in a cell with someone in a California prison means your loyalty is to that person and it's you both against the prison world. From there for each race, someone represents the entire building. From there someone for each race has the most influence for the entire yard. Without this structure, chaos usually ensues and the lack of control causes problems for everyone. With this system there is always a ton of pressure to run things the right way. Rules and regulations are constantly tailored and redefined, with violence solving every problem. Without the violence, there isn't any respect. With the violence, someone or a select group coordinates it. Because of the violence, there is constant pressure. I realized a way to deal with it. "If it comes to that we'll tell the southern Mexicans what's happening and come up with a mutual solution."

Giant asked, "What do you have in mind?"

I was already thinking of the two southern Mexicans I would talk to and said, "We'll have to tell them that it is in both of our best interest to not allow it to happen."

Giant asked, "How can we control it if the prison administration tries to put us in a southern Mexican cell or vice versa?"

"By not going in the cell. Instead, we or the southern Mexican refuses the move."

Giant asked, "What would happen?"

"It would force the administration's hand to recognize they have us labeled wrong."

Giant asked, "Where would they put us?"

"Back in solitary."

Chapter 20 The Inmate Classification Committee Hearing

A month into our solitary confinement our cell was called for I.C.C. I went first and walked to the office in handcuffs. The Warden held my right arm and guided me in the door. There was a large oak table with a collection of people sitting down staring at me like I wasn't human. At the head of the table, staring at all the files in front of him was a light colored Black man with reading glasses. Next to him were Lieutenant Pickler and two other White men. The Warden led me to a seat facing the prison administration and left.

The Black man looked up for a second and said, "Sit down inmate Johnson. I'm Counselor Moon. This is Lieutenant Pickler, Inmate Gang Investigator Moore and Doctor Brennan from Health Services."

Counselor Moon looked back at my file and fingered through more pages like he wasn't ready to begin. Lieutenant Pickler was the only one in uniform and he was staring at me like he was enjoying the moment. Like he already had a plan worked out for my destiny. The other two at the desk blended in as if they were just taking notes.

Counselor Moon's reading glasses moved up and down his nose while he studied my file. He found the page he wanted and looked up at me. "Inmate Johnson, who do you run with in prison?"

I answered right away. "I'm a White inmate, not a southern Mexican."

Counselor Moon's glasses flexed up his nose and his forehead creased into a skeptical look like he didn't believe me. He said, "Why did you get involved in that riot?"

I couldn't answer the unwritten code of silence. If I said too much and it became a written report, I would be looked at like a rat or informant.

Counselor Moon shook his head and said, "In your file it says you were a cartel level gun and drug dealer. That leads me to believe you're affiliated with the Mexicans. Your involvement in this riot leads me to believe your affiliation is with the southern Mexicans. Are you a south sider or a Sureno?"

I knew that both were considered prison gangs under the heading of the Mexican Mafia. The Mexican street gangs all over southern California merged into one of those two headings in prison. I answered, "I'm a White man and I don't claim any gangs."

Counselor Moon snorted and said, "That's hard to believe."

Lieutenant Pickler jumped in and said, "We're going to have to assume you're a southern Mexican."

Investigator Moore asked, "Does he have any gang tattoos? Maybe something related to the number 13?"

Lieutenant Pickler responded, "He doesn't have any tattoos at all but considering his crimes on the street and involvement in this riot, I think he's a sleeper for the Mexican Mafia."

I looked at the collection of faces. They were all nodding their heads solemnly in agreement. The feeling of doom was setting in. I imagined the worst case scenario. I could be stuck in solitary for years, for the rest of my sentence.

Investigator Moore added, "That would be a Mexican Mafia tactic, to have someone on the inside with the Whites as a drug dealer and collector."

Counselor Moon said, "We are clearing you for program in solitary but are considering you a southern Mexican inmate. You will go to yard with them and be housed in a cell with them."

I almost lost it in frustration and found myself ready to give up the code of silence. I wrestled with it in my thoughts, if I explained myself without implicating anyone...

I said, "You know the policies at this prison related to space. You know that different races use different showers and sides of the dayroom and yard. All we did is defend ourselves. How does that make me a southern Mexican?"

I knew it wasn't enough. I also knew that being stuck in solitary for a lot longer was now my destiny. I studied Counselor Moon. He was shaking his head. Lieutenant Pickler cocked his head back with a smug look on his face like he was enjoying my position even more. He said, "No other White inmates got involved in the riot on the entire yard, except you two."

I looked at the Inmate Gang Investigator. He was staring at one of my files and taking notes. This wasn't getting any better. I looked at the Doctor and felt like I needed a check up from the neck up.

I got back to the cell and it was Giant's turn. While he was going through the strip search he asked, "What happened? Why do you look so focused?"

I said, "They have me labeled as a southern Mexican now. It's all bad."

Giant put on the jumpsuit and backed his way to the open tray slot. He bent over and stuck his wrist through the opening and looked into my eyes. He asked, "What should I do?"

A possible answer came to me. "Hit up the Warden on the walk to the office. Maybe he can help us."

For the next 20 minutes I paced the length of the cell back and forth like a locomotive. There was room to take 4 steps each way. Walking fast and turning on a dime at each end helped me think. To avoid the darkness of depression I thought about something good. We were getting cleared for yard for 10 hours a week. Solitary hell would be much easier to deal with.

I watched Giant walk back to the cell with his hands cuffed behind his back. He was hunched over and still almost a foot taller than the Warden. He looked like he was losing it. The Warden held his right shoulder. I heard Giant asking, "How am I a southern Mexican when I'm a White man from northern California? This crap is ridiculous!"

The Warden looked very confused. It didn't look like he was going to be able to give us a quick fix. Giant was so perturbed that it looked like he had to see the Warden's face. Bent over in a hunch already, he turned his neck and head to look at the Warden.

The Warden tried to avoid the issue and put his other arm in the air to signal the tower guard to pop the cell.

The cell popped open and Giant walked in. The Warden quickly slammed the cell shut and put his key in the tray slot. Giant didn't turn around. Instead, he looked at the Warden through the Plexiglas and said calmly and slowly, "Warden Parker I'm a White inmate from San Francisco. That's northern California. They just labeled me a southern Mexican so now I'm going to be stuck in solitary confinement for way longer."

It looked like the Warden cared. His face had a pained look like he was frustrated. He asked, "How would that keep you in solitary confinement?"

Giant said, "Because when I finally get finished with my solitary time for this riot I'm going to refuse to get housed being labeled a southern Mexican."

It looked like the Warden was beginning to understand how deep the racial issue was. I asked, "Warden, why aren't you at the head of the table for the inmate Classification Committee? Why are you out here doing the grunt work of escorting inmates?"

The question stunned the Warden. His confused look turned into an authentic look and he answered, "I just transferred to this prison."

That evening we heard the vestibule door grind open. An army of 8 prison guards entered the building. The tower guard tapped on the microphone and announced, "Shower time! From now on you will get showers 3 times a week. We have more prison staff. Since we don't have much time tonight you only get 10 minutes."

Chapter 22 Yard business

For yard we were only allowed to wear our boxer shorts, a white shirt and flip flops. We went through the strip search and backed up to get handcuffed. We walked to a door that opened to a narrow concrete path that went for 30 feet to the yards. The sunlight blinded me after not being out of our cell for a month and I had to walk slower to let my eyes adjust.

We walked the path that led to two mini yards. Each yard was about the size of a half court for basketball. There was a 10 foot high fence around it and razor wire in swirls at the top. In place of a tower, above the yard, was a steel catwalk with two prison guards holding guns. The escort guards led us into our yard. It started with a separate boxed in fenced area about the size of a bathroom. We got our handcuffs released through the tray slot and one of the guards asked, "Do you want to use some clippers to cut your hair or trim your beard?"

We needed some man grooming in a desperate way and used the clippers to make us as close to bald headed as possible. My facial hair had turned into an out of control goatee and I removed as much as I could. While we played barber on each other the southern Mexican inmates started to arrive.

Pericho and Sureno walked with their backs straight and their chests sticking out as far as possible. I almost laughed out loud but instead thought about how sad it was. They were a couple of 18 year olds who desperately didn't want to look weak. The guards unlocked the first cage in the mini yard next to ours and they walked in. Pericho was the crazier one with wild eyes and a bald head with scars in multiple places. As soon as he got his handcuffs off he took his shirt off.

After we finished grooming ourselves we entered our mini yard. There was a basketball hoop on one end that faced the other mini yard 6 feet away. On the other end of the yard there was a shower head and a toilet. I noticed a basketball in the corner and got it. Giant and I took turns shooting free throws and watched all the southern Mexicans walk in handcuffs to the yard cages.

One by one they got their handcuffs off and entered the yard. One of the guards decided to put the inmates from the bottom floor in our yard and the inmates from the top floor went into the other one. The younger inmates all took their shirts off as soon as the handcuffs were removed and I realized it was in defiance. They weren't going to let anyone tell them they had to wear a shirt to cover neighborhood tattoos. I saw Johny get his handcuffs removed and he walked toward us with his shirt on. He looked different, like his outlook on life wasn't as positive. Maybe it was that all hope of ever getting a chance to parole on a life sentence was gone.

He stopped in front of us and forced a smile. Giant was so happy to see him he gave him an immediate hug. I followed up with one next and asked, "Are you alright?"

The love from both Giant and I brought back a little spark to Johny's smile and he nodded his head. He said, "Thank you for helping us out."

It hit me that maybe he was also depressed that he'd killed another person. Even though it was self defense, it probably had him thinking about how he'd committed himself to being in that position his whole life. I encouraged him, "Johny you protected your people and couldn't avoid it."

I looked him right in the eyes and his were brown pools of sorrow. He broke the eye lock and looked at the ground and nodded his head. Our attention was broken by a distraction on the other mini yard.

"Hey Johny!"

There were over 20 inmates on each of the mini yards and almost everyone stopped what they were doing to watch. The man who called Johny was Topo. He was staring at us from the other mini yard with his hands holding the fence. He looked like a Mexican Joe Pesci. He took off his white shirt and from his waist to his neck there was a collection of tattoo art. His usually bald head had a little hair on it and it made his widow's peak more prominent. We watched Johny walk to the fence. He grabbed it with his hands like Topo was doing and stood almost a foot taller looking down.

I looked at Giant. He noticed the difference in Johny also. He said, "He's changed. Even his voice is deeper."

I nodded my head and noticed all the southern Mexicans on both of the mini yards begin to establish positions. They were all somewhat watching Johny and Topo like they were waiting for orders. They constantly looked over at the two elders and then went back to whatever they were doing.

Johny nodded his head to Topo and turned and walked to us. His expression was even harder and I realized what it was. While I knew him on the mainline prison yard before the riot, he was himself due to the lack of heavy politics. Now in Administrative Segregation heavy politics were being forced on him.

The pep in his step was gone. He looked up at us while deep in thought and forced a smile and asked, "You guys want to work out with us?"

I felt my expression harden on my face over the stress of our situation. I nodded my head and said, "Sure... We need to see if you can help us figure something out after..."

Johny nodded his head and it was obvious he already knew it was over us being labeled and housed as southern Mexicans. I realized in that instant that every southern Mexican on both yards was aware. None of them had even greeted us. There were a handful of southerners that had looked up to us and loved talking to us on the mainline. Now they were avoiding us.

I heard Topo get everyone's attention in Spanish slang and understood him. He yelled out, "Excuse me, attention brothers! It's time for our workout. Everyone line up!"

Johny nodded his head to us and said, "We'll help you figure it out after we exercise."

He quickly got into his role as leader on our mini yard and shuffled all of the southern Mexicans into a line. Giant and I maintained our positions and backed up to melt into the line forming around us. Our backs were to the fence and we were facing the gun tower catwalk above us. I looked up for the first time on the yard and noticed that both guards were studying the dynamics of how all the inmates were congregating with intensity. It was easy to see and understand that Topo was running one yard and Johny was running the other one. Both Topo and Johny had their backs to the tower guards while we were all facing them. It had to look like we were a part of the southern Mexican army.

Topo called out the cadence in Spanish and I understood it.

"One hundred jumping jacks...Ready Begin!"

We did the jumping jacks.

Topo yelled, "Fifty squats...Ready Begin!"

We did the squats.

Topo yelled, "Fifty pushups...Ready begin!"

We did the pushups.

Topo yelled, "Southern Mexicans!! How do you feel?"

Everyone, including Giant and I, yelled, "One hundred percent!"

Our exercises continued for 45 more minutes. When we finished Topo came back to the fence and called Johny to talk to him. Giant and I watched the two communicate and waited for them to call us over. We both looked at the two tower guards.

Giant said, "This doesn't look good."

I looked my friend right in the eyes. His were confused pools of blue ocean water. I joked, "Where's your Mexican pride?"

I got the desired laugh out of him and watched his face get softer. We turned our attention back to Johny and Topo. They talked for 20 more minutes and waved us over.

Topo stood holding the fence with both of his hands and I studied his tattoo art. He had LA in dark ink blasted in block letters on his chest. The rest of the art was a depiction of his gangland upbringing in east LA. I looked into his dark brown eyes and they were almost void of any emotion. He was staring into my eyes and it was a sign of respect that he was dealing with me on the matter. He said, "First and foremost my thanks go to both of you for helping us in the riot."

I nodded my head and said, "No problem. You and Johny are our friends."

Topo looked at Giant and nodded his head.

Giant said, "Your welcome. We weren't going to just stand there and let you guys get outnumbered."

We stood there staring at each other and neither Johny nor Topo said anything. I let what seemed like an eternity pass and said, "We have a problem. We're being housed and labeled as southern Mexicans."

There wasn't any shock on Topo's face. He was a stoic warrior who I knew had already given our situation a lot of thought. It began to dawn on me how deep our problem was. The southern Mexican politics in prison could be looked at like a mafia battle that incorporated up to 500 southern California street gangs. Not to mention their business with all of the cartels from Mexico. With all of that to deal with the pressure on all of them was enormous. They surely heard our problem discussed through the vent and heard Giant vehemently telling the Warden he wasn't a southern Mexican. Maybe they felt insulted.

Topo nodded his head and said, "This is your ticket to enter if you want it?"

I realized that he was offering us his blessing to become southern Mexicans. Maybe the I.G.I guard at classification had that part of it right. That it was a Mexican Mafia tactic to recruit White inmates. I felt Giant looking at me to say something. I didn't feel any pressure at all. I had never wanted to be a gang member or join a group to feel protected or part of another family. I made a show of looking at my arm and said, "I'm White and I'm not a gang member. So thanks for the offer but I think we make better friends."

As soon as I finished I realized that Johny's body posture relaxed. I looked at him and saw that authentic smile I remembered. I looked at Giant next.

There was a silent expectation building to hear what he had to say. Topo stared into his eyes. Johny turned toward him as well.

Giant stood there a foot and a half taller than Topo. I realized with his hair shaved down to the scalp he looked even more intimidating. I imagined him as a southern Mexican being used as a soldier to earn his points. He would never be able to break free and would spend the rest of his life in prison. He nodded his head to Topo and said, "Thanks for the offer Topo but I want to go home on my parole date in just under a year."

Topo's stoic expression didn't waver. He nodded his head and said, "No problem. I can respect that."

Now that we had the preliminaries out of the way I was curious to see how he and Johny would problem solve it. Johny got the ball rolling. He said, "When you get done with this SHU term in Solitary the next prison is going to send you to a southern Mexican's cell. If you go in the cell it will be a big headache. Imagine if there are tensions with another race already on the yard you pull up too? What if one of the White inmates on the yard owes us a bunch of money for dope? Or what if there is a war brewing with the Black inmates?"

I thought about the level of secrecy the southern Mexicans held together with all of their gangs and issues. Having a White inmate in the cell would disrupt that.

Topo pointed out the problem even further. He said, "Plus you will have a hard time explaining to the rest of your White people why you are in a southern Mexican cell."

I thought about it. If the wrong White people were in power on the next yard we landed on, they might shun us.

Topo said, "I'm not telling you what to do, but I wouldn't go in a southern cell and let the door close on you."

Giant said, "Refuse to get housed?"

Both Topo and Johny nodded their heads. Topo said, "But that is where your problems really start. Once you refuse to go in a cell think about how that will look to all of the southern Mexicans and all of the White inmates?"

I couldn't believe I hadn't thought of it! The next prison would be like all the others. As soon as we got there the politics would began. An inmate would be in charge of studying all of the new arrivals to find out if they were a child molester, rapist or informant. They would ask for our criminal history paperwork. Not locking up was going to make us look like we had something to hide in a big way.

I shook my head in disgust at our positon and asked, "What do you suggest?"

Topo said, "Me and Johny's names are well known. We'll write a message for you to give to the southern Mexicans. That will take care of you at that level and it will actually work out well for you. The message will circulate up the chain of command to the shot callers. All the southerners will know you did us a favor and had our backs. How you deal with the Whites is on you."

I realized that a message from both Topo and Johny would save us a lot of explaining. It dawned on me that our criminal history paperwork wasn't in our cell right now. It had been boxed up and stored somewhere after the riot. All we had was the paperwork related to the riot. It would be enough to start with.

Johny filled in the rest of the blanks. He said, "You both better take our messages and your riot paperwork and wrap them up as small and tight as you can in plastic to wear out of here."

What he was saying was to stick the paperwork up our asses and carry it to the next prison. Our property wouldn't come with us to our next cell. Instead it would go through a search at the next prison for up to a month after we were cleared for the mainline.

Chapter 23 These Are the Prison Days of our Lives

The next two months flew by. With yard on one day, and showers on the following day, it was easier to get into a routine that didn't crawl by as painfully. Giant and I got our messages from Topo and Johny. I knew Johny was well known in the Orange County gang world so it would help. On the yard Johny told me that Topo's name was one of the biggest in southern California. We folded and rolled all the paperwork up into a thumb sized package. Every day for a week we took the plastic wrap off our lunch sandwiches and wrapped it around our paperwork package. We coordinated with our neighbor's in the cell above us and got what we needed to make a homemade lighter to seal the plastic wrap around our paperwork. By taking a couple of razors apart, we stuck each metal piece of blade into the electrical outlet. With pencil lead touching both metal pieces a flame was created. We sealed up what we started calling, "Our insurance package" every day to make sure it didn't come unraveled while it was inside us.

The same two investigators who threatened us with outside charges with the District Attorney came back in. Two new legal counselors also came along side of them to advise us of our rights. The good news was that the District Attorney wasn't filing charges on anyone. The two legal counselors explained that the reports for our building established that the southerners were the ones under attack so everything was considered self defense. There still wasn't anyway to beat the state charges for "participating in the group melee-riot". We were all given small SHU terms that by now were almost served.

We went to another I.C.C hearing and both Giant and I tried to get back to White man status to no avail. Instead, they told Giant he would be transferring to Folsom State Prison. They told me I would be transferring to the new Soledad Prison called Salinas Valley. These are the prison days of our lives.

Excerpt for Underdog
~*~Underdog~*~
"That which doesn't kill you makes you stronger...But if you're just getting stronger and going in the wrong direction you're just getting more lost..."
~*~*~*~

Chapter 1: Animal Cruelty
My wife, Annette, and I walked into the shelter and a putrid odor assaulted us. Mr. Robinson, the current owner of The Animal House, a non-profit shelter for abandoned and abused canines, turned on the light. With the light came the noise. Over 50 dogs started barking and I listened carefully. There was a mixture of angry and violent barking, combined with some fearful and desperate howling.
The small barn the dogs were housed in was packed. It was overcapacity. There were two rows of cages with a 4'

walkway down the middle for about 30'. The first steel cage was 6' long and 2' high and contained a group of dogs fighting for space. They were packed into the cages like sardines without an inch to spare. Poodles, Beagles, Collies and some mixed breeds bumped, jumped and jockeyed for position to get as close to us as possible. Their floor was filled with scraps of old newspapers and I realized where the odor came from. The newspapers were soiled with their excrement. Poop and piss. I looked at my wife to see if she noticed. She did. Her thick brown hair flew in an arc over her tiny face as she whipped her gaze at me. Her turquoise green eyes, shaped like almonds, focused all of her energy at me to do something.

I looked at the man trying to understand if he was a slum lord for dogs, or if he was really trying to help them. Mr. Robinson was overweight and unkempt. His posture radiated a lazy, not too interested in other people countenance. His face looked like a walrus with baggy hanging jowls, covered by a peppering of brown beard that matched the hair on his head, and resembled dust balls behind the refrigerator. I asked, "Why do you make them live in their own shit and piss?"

Mr. Robinson gave me a stare and then a glare. Like that was going to scare me. It pissed me off so I asked, "How would you like it if I put you in that cage to sleep in that filth?"

It looked like Mr. Robinson had decided that I could and would. His face changed into a defensive smirk and he quipped, "I don't have any help around here. I can't do it all alone!"

I looked to my wife. It was her turn. She kicked one of her legs out in an aggressive and sexy posture and exploded with a litany, "I bet you're really good at raising money from the public as if you take care of dogs! You better hire someone or do the work yourself, or the County will shut you down."

As usual, my wife nailed it and got to the root of the problem. A week ago we started looking for a dog or two on the internet. The Animal House didn't look like this. Mr. Robinson must have been using someone else's pictures from a shelter that actually groomed dogs for new homes. These dogs didn't have any hope. We turned our attention to the rest of the confined cages. It got worse fast.

We started walking slowly, now my wife and I were leading the way. There were six more cages in both rows housing multiple canines like the first cage, but the last one had a cage on top of a cage and I stopped. Fecal matter and strips of wet newspaper hung from the top cage in sections where the bottom opened a tiny bit. The small dogs in the cage beneath looked even meaner than the other dogs because they had the poop and piss dried up on their coats of hair. I almost lost it, but instead got into action. I picked up the cage and walked it past Mr. Robinson forcing him to jump out of the way as I walked out the barn. The barn opened up into a fenced in area and I set the cage down next to a bunch of dog leashes hanging from the fence. After all the dogs were leashed to the fence, an appropriate distance from each other, I walked back into the barn.

"Mr. Robinson, clean the cage and wash them while we pick out a couple of our new watch dogs." My wife smiled at me and we walked deeper into the barn. Now, the big dogs were in the last five cages of single celled animals. I looked at both rows and wanted all ten dogs. My wife said, "I want every dog here BJ."

"I know honey, but we can only take two."

I studied my wife and saw her razor sharp brain operating. She was going to figure out a way to have them all. She had her foot down in that way that said she wasn't budging. I helped her figure it out. "Baby, the only way to rescue all of the dogs from this fraudulent dog rescuer is to take over his operation. Until we figure that out we can only take two."

That seemed to satisfy her because she lifted her foot from the stubborn stance and pivoted to look at the rest of the dogs.

I studied the larger dogs. There was a Great Dane, three German shepherds', four mixed breeds, a rottweiler and a pit bull. The rottweiler was the biggest beast, built long and low to the ground. His face wore an expression of abuse. I looked closer and realized his last owner had branded his forehead. The fur had been replaced with a tattoo in the shape of a lightning bolt. The pit bull had the same lightning bolt markings over his pug nose. Annette looked at all the large dogs and said, "I know which two you want?"
"How?"
"I know you. You want the ones that nobody else will take. The rottweiler and the pit."
"You know me pretty well missy."
"Do these caged animals remind you of the time you spent in prison honey?"
They did. I had spent over ten years in a variety of California Level 4 prisons during my drug addicted and dealing years where I raged against the system. Now, in recovery from my addictions and old, ingrained behaviors, my goal was to help other prisoners find a new life outside of prison walls.
Later today, I was taking a trip to the most notorious prison in California, Pelican Bay, to visit my friend Damon Smith, AKA Rott. Damon had followed my path, by dealing marijuana while it was still illegal in the 1990's, he also got caught up in California's overzealous determination to label him a gang member. We had both done time on some dangerously violent prison yards and keeping the peace for our White race at times called for violence just to survive. Unlike me, Damon had peppered his body with tattoos. Those same tattoos combined with the prison violations for violence, were the reasons he was in the Pelican Bay Security Housing Unit, also known as the SHU, or also commonly referred to as Super-Max. Lost in my thoughts, I noticed my wife studying me.
Annette said, "Honey I know you were probably in over a hundred different cages like the ones these dogs are in

but you made it. Having lived through it, what would you say are the most important things that need to happen to help other prisoners make the change into good role models?"

That was the million dollar question, but actually, how can you put a price on a human being..? I thought about how I turned it around. My Spiritual connection to God started it by realizing that even if nobody else in the world loved me, God did. If everyone else accused me, God forgave me. Back then, sitting in a cell for the umpteenth time feeling this wisdom wash over me, I focused on finding a way to turn everything I'd been through into a blessing.

I smiled at my wife and answered, "The first thing is love. It's just like with these dogs, if you love them they will be the most loyal friends you could ever have. The next stage is direction. The prisoners need a way to put all their energy in a positive direction. The next vitally important step is faith. Once the prisoners or released prisoners see that other people believe in them, that they too can benefit the community, find employment, have a family and fit in, they will start believing a life in a fruitful direction is possible. When all this happens, hope opens up new doors. The reason 7 out of 10 released California prisoners return back to prison within three years is because they have no hope."

My wife smiled at me in a loving way and then turned her attention back to the dogs. She was thinking about how to rescue all of them again.

She said, "Go visit your friend Damon in Pelican Bay and offer him some hope. I'm going to figure out how to give these dogs some."

I knew how she could do it. She had battled addiction while I was in prison and found recovery after she got involved in a support group for women, the Ashland Angel House. When I got out of prison we united and got married. Now she devoted her time to helping other women get back on their feet until they could get their kids back... She might be able to get the women at the

Ashland Angel House to help these dogs, and at the same time help themselves by being needed and fortifying some self worth...

Chapter 2: A Drive Down Memory Lane

Pelican Bay State Prison was a fourteen hour drive from Orange County, California and the 5 Freeway North gave me plenty of time to think about my friend Damon, and why the California Prison system was trying to validate him as a gang member and keep him housed in the Super-Max SHU.

A number of years ago we had both been housed on a volatile Level 4 prison where the Whites were the minority. We only had 8% of the population. The Mexican inmates made up about 40% and the Blacks another 40%. The Asians made up the rest. For about a year and a half the Mexican and Black inmates fought each other in skirmishes with prison made weapons in riots that brought a handful of casualties. It had started in the gym where prisoners lived on bunk beds with hardly an inch to spare. The Mexican prisoners pushed the rules and regulations a little too hard with things like which toilets and showers each race was to use and it caused problems with the Black prisoners. The Black prisoners decided enough was enough and took the initiative. About forty Black prisoners jumped the Mexicans with just fist and feet. They won the first battle. The Mexicans won round 2 with prison made knives and we had a serious battle underway. The war had gone back and forth with one race of inmates attacking the other with a three month lockdown in between.

It looked like it was finally coming to an end, but just before it did; the Prison Gang Coordinators took the two strongest leaders for the Mexicans, L'il Bird and Boxer, off the yard by labeling them Mexican Mafia. Whether they were or not wasn't my call but I did acknowledge them as good leaders. With them on the yard, Damon and I had developed a good program and established a safe policy for our separate races to get along. Now, without their presence the rest of the Mexicans fought each other to fill the void to control the yard for their stake and it was up in the air whether or not the policies we had in place with the former shot callers would hold. During this process some of our White race started running drugs for the Mexicans without anybody keeping a regulated eye on them.

This is what happened...

The Yard was at full capacity, which meant that all of the Mexican and Blacks were back on the yard and off lock down and getting full program. That left a very small area for the White inmates to congregate on the yard. There were twelve concrete tables and we had 1 as our share to view the yard and put our heads together. Damon and I had come up with a strategy to keep the White inmates united and on the same page as much as possible for the safety of the entire unit, with a protective eye on the youngsters. Our aim was to focus on the potential for problems and to take preventive measures to keep a race war from happening.

In prison, perception is reality. You have to handle your business with precision to maintain honor. As a whole, if your race or gang looks weak, like there is a kink in the armor, it invites every vulture, shark and piranha on the yard to the feast. With this in mind, we authored a program on paper that was sent to every White inmate's cell to establish some rules and regulations. We only asked that every member of our race show up to yard to show solidarity, to work out to show honor and to respect everyone at all times.

Our drug debt and alcohol policy was one of zero tolerance but how can you control another's addiction? The rule was, don't get high if it can make other people die. Dope and alcohol were to be purchased, "Off the shelf", which meant with store items owned on your shelf. No fronts or loans. Most of the drug transactions in prison that bring violence and death are done with money order payouts and when a race isn't paid someone has to get stabbed to cover the bill. We had just found out that a White inmate had done $550 of heroin from the Mexicans, as if he could pay it. He couldn't, putting every other White man on the yard in jeopardy of a war against the Mexicans. We were outnumbered over 15 to 1. The Mexicans were counting on the bill being paid with a money order mailed out from the streets. That money was going to fund another shipment of dope into prison.

I had another problem. My parole date was days away and part of me wanted to tuck my tail and avoid this issue. The other part of me knew I wasn't going to stop being me. The years of prison life had molded me into a leader and my survival and pride were tied to how I'd faced things. I couldn't let it go.

Damon and I had finished our workout routine in our usual spot by our buried swords in the back corner of the yard where we sat on the curb to survey things when Blockhead, a fellow White man walked up looking serious.

"Hey brothers, I have some bad news."

Blockhead further explained how "Lefty", a White man and our responsibility, ran up the drug debt for heroin. It was hard to pay attention to Blockhead because Damon and I were watching three of the newest Mexican power brokers while they walked the yard. There was Termite, one of the Mexicans who was trying to call shots, but was more of a drug smuggler and the current big connection for heroin. There was Cyclone, a straight gang banging killer, who also had aspirations to take over and call shots, but was too young and lacked the experience. The third Mexican went by Stranger from West Los Angeles. We deduced Stranger as the one who would take over. I didn't like him. He was all about posturing, without enough conscience.

Stranger was walking by us with Cyclone on his right and Termite on his left when we heard Stranger say just loud enough, "I got the yard for the Mexicans now and I want you to be my mouthpiece Cyclone."

Cyclone was out of his element as a yard politician. A murderous rage flowed through his blood and his instincts were on edge. He didn't say anything because he couldn't. He'd already told all his "homeboys" that the yard was his. All of his "homeboys" in San Bernardino would think he was a joke if he became Stranger's puppet. The whole territory and every other Mexican with a 13 tattooed on their body would laugh at him.
Stranger knew that Cyclone had asserted that he had the keys to the yard and was calling shots. He also knew that Cyclone had squeezed in on Termite for a cut of his dope. Having more experience, he knew that it was put up or shut up time and stopped walking. Both Termite and Cyclone were caught off guard and kept walking a few paces then stopped, both with confused looks on their faces, they turned to look at Stranger.
Stranger said, "Termite from this point on a third of the dope you bring in goes to me to run the yard." Termite nodded his head, he was fine with that and it looked like he was thinking about how Stranger had just got to the yard recently from where he'd left the biggest mobsters in Southern California at Palm Hall, the most notorious section of Chino prison, where most of the inmates were waiting for a bus ride to the Pelican Bay SHU, and what that implied.
Cyclone stared at Stranger with so much uncomfortable energy flooding through his veins he was shaking, on the edge of aiming that force against Stranger just to get it over with.
Stranger, Termite and Cyclone were within twenty feet from us.
I got up and walked towards the three Mexicans, keeping ten feet between us. I felt their energy and zeroed in on Cyclone. His hands were balled up in fist and they were still trembling.
I watched Stranger's eyes drop and notice Cyclone on the verge. He avoided the fight by cutting the tension with me as the distraction. He said, "What's up BJ?"

I realized if I hadn't gotten up they would have been going at it in a fight over their internal power struggle, maybe it wasn't too late, "You guys look busy. Let me talk to you when you're done."

It was in that moment I picked Stranger to fight if diplomacy broke down and peace wasn't possible. The energy vibrating off Cyclone was palpable and familiar to me, it said, my childhood was so wrong that I would rather die than not live up to my own expectations. Cyclone finally looked at me. His dark brown eyes were void but there was an internal dialogue going through his brain that could change them back to rage in a nanosecond.

It appeared Stranger knew he'd just avoided a trip to the hole over a yard fight, temporarily, and played another move to distract Cyclone. "Cyclone do you want to talk to BJ?"

Cyclone's mind flooded with impulses unsure of what to do...."No." It looked like Stranger realized the best move was to get into action before the tension hit a crescendo again so he waved at me to have the talk with him. Stranger's eyes never left Cyclone and he tried to continue to command the situation. He nodded at Cyclone and said, "I'll get at you when I'm done."

I watched Stranger take a few steps into the yard for privacy leaving Cyclone and Termite on the track. He'd been doing this all his life and it showed, but it was all posturing. He wasn't a made guy yet. I positioned myself so I was facing the gun tower with Stranger in between and with Damon sitting on the curb to the right. To keep my vantage point the way I wanted, I kept the ten foot gap between Stranger and me.

Stranger was still waiting for Cyclone and Termite to leave and walk the track but they were still standing there like they didn't know what to do.

I broke through Stranger's lack of attention on me by saying loud enough for Damon, Cyclone and Termite to hear, "Stranger are you who I talk to for the Mexicans? I want to make sure you know what has already been established between our two races for our drug policy." Stranger's face flashed toward me. All the tension from his power struggle with Cyclone was now facing me head on. His dark brown eyes creased into a frown, angry soldier. He took a step toward me to close the gap, postured and asked in a quiet voice meant for us, "Do you always talk so loud?"

I glanced at the gun tower guard, 50 yards away and 100' in the air, poised with his rifle. He was watching. Then I smiled to break the tension and said in a quiet voice, "I had something worked out with L'il Bird before he left. I need you to get at him to verify it but take my word for it now and implement it, $180 off the shelf dope policy. I heard Lefty owes Termite $550."

Stranger looked confused, like I was speaking a foreign language.

I didn't hesitate to help him understand. "Come on Stranger, you've been around. Drug debts get out of hand without a policy, 180 off the shelf max. That way dope fiends can't cause our two races problems."

Cyclone and Termite finally walked away. Stranger's eyes followed their path along the track until they were under the gun tower and then looked back at me. "I know what you mean but I have to get at L'il Bird in the hole first."

That was going to take too long. I needed Stranger to run the yard with an iron fist for the Mexicans to keep the problem with drug debts from delivering chaos before it was too late.

It didn't look like Stranger was up to the challenge so I urged him in the right direction, "Come on hommie, you know what's up. We have to handle our business faster than that. Why don't you take my word for it while you get at L'il Bird to confirm it and I'll deal with it on my end by getting as much of the $180 from Lefty before he gets dealt with?"

By now, Cyclone and Termite were all the way down the track by Building 5 and circling it past our White table. I noticed Damon was watching them.

Stranger nodded his head as if he agreed with me but said, "Nope, I need that $550 Lefty owes and if you had that $180 policy worked out with L'il Bird I'll consider implementing that policy then, when I find that out. It's my yard for the Mexicans now, L'il Bird is gone."

For the rest of the day it was a delicate balance to figure out how to deal with things. Our White race was used to dealing with the policy already in place regarding drug debts so we couldn't ask them to cover the $550 bill. Doing so would have made us look bendable. Like we were made of money and any kind of pressure would separate us from it. We bounced around the idea that we could collect a small amount of the money from each White inmate until the $550 was covered but realized that would have been sending the wrong precedence. That would have sent the message to the rest of the White inmates that it was okay to run up a drug debt like Lefty had, because the whole race would just kick in to cover it...

Chapter 3: Prison Politics

The next morning was a scorcher in the desert sun. Now that the yard was off lockdown the walk through the building and vestibule to get to the yard was crowded. Bodies of every skin color rushed their way out to get to desired locations on the yard.

When we made it out the vestibule I noticed that our building was opening first and Damon and I were the only ones wearing state prison issue denim jackets buttoned up tight over denim jeans over boots. Every other inmate was in casual clothes from their packages like shorts, tank tops and tennis shoes. If the guards and gun tower were paying attention, this was the first sign. Damon went toward Building 1 just to the right and I walked to our White table in front of Building 5 to the left. I walked past Building 3 right as the vestibule door opened and a sea of inmates came charging out, in a hurry to get to the work out bars, a card game or some other plan, like look for dope. I walked past Building 4 and the same thing happened. I got to our table and stared at Building 5 where Stranger would be coming out. The vestibule door hadn't opened yet; the intake building always took longer to release.

I sat on top of the table and waited. By now the yard had over four hundred inmates congregating into sections near the workout bars, basketball court and handball court. I found Damon walking with Jason, Lefty's cell mate, and both of them carried a negative energy, even worse than it should have been.

Damon got to the table and said, "Lefty overdosed last night."

I didn't have time to register that fact. The action sped up and there wasn't time to think. The vestibule door to Building 5 opened.

As expected Stranger walked through the vestibule door first and just the way he walked offended me. He was dressed in all state issue blue denim like we were. He had his hands in his jacket as if he might have a knife in there. I got off the table and walked toward him but so did a couple of Mexicans from their table. I thought quick and realized it would work out better if I let them talk to him first. I stood off to the side and pretended to stretch on the edge of the track so I wouldn't be so obvious and gave myself an angle to study the yard to see where the White inmates were.

The two Mexicans were done with Stranger and I let them walk past me and cut Stranger off. "Hey stud I need to talk to you."

Stranger looked too sure of himself, like things were working out for him as the shot caller, and he tried to brush me off like I was an insignificant problem he'd already resolved. He looked at me like a peon and said; "Not now BJ I have to handle some shit."

I usually don't give someone I'd decided was an enemy a chance but I felt my rage boiling and knew he didn't have a chance either way so I did what I rarely do, talk, "You need to handle this dope policy, last chance."

I was six feet away from Stranger and looked for Damon and found him. He was walking toward me as fast as he could about a hundred feet away. Close enough.

I looked back at Stranger. He looked shocked. Like it was too hard for him to believe I wasn't bending to his will.

I didn't wait for a response and rushed him. Instead of trying to knock him out with a punch, I used my right knee in an explosive upper thrust. It caught him flush in his right leg and his body folded inward forcing his two hands in front of his face to come down. I fired a right handed bomb that bounced off his forehead because he shuffled backward to not go down from my knee chop but it was too late for him. I was on top of him raining down punches and crowding in on him until we were both on the ground. I leveraged myself on top of him and hammered punches into his face like a piston a few times until he bucked me off. I landed with my hands in front of me and popped back up and got to him before he made it all the way up and timed a kick to his face that sent him back to the ground.

I charged him again but was met by a sea of other Mexicans. In the heat of the moment I knew they had launched themselves from their table and everywhere else nearby as one unit. I was barely able to see peripherally. The noise of yells, bodies running and the sounds of punches reached my ears and fear almost took over. I utilized that fear and fired both fists in hyper drive. My punches were the only thing clearing the way as I felt and saw Mexicans coming at me from the side for cheap shots. Their blows were landing but I only heard the thumps and didn't feel them from the effects of adrenaline.

I found Damon's head bobbing a little higher than the rest and remembered the plan. I punched both of my fists as straight and fast as I could to get space. Little by little separation occurred and I could see things. Damon ended up right where he was supposed to be and for a second, we had our backs locked against each other impossible to surround, then, we turned our bodies so we could both shuffle backwards until we felt the side of the building behind us.

The noise of the battle came back to me. I heard all the usual sounds; the alarm, the block guns, the orders from guards, "Get down! Get down!" I felt my second wind, more adrenaline and the need to help other White inmates take over my being. My vision adjusted with my back safe and I continued distributing punches and knocking the smaller Mexicans down. Damon was doing the same thing next to me and we had enough space to see a cluster of White inmates getting outnumbered and pummeled fifty feet away.

One of our youngest was too small for the Mexicans and I saw one smash his head from behind and he crumpled to the ground with over twenty Mexicans stomping and kicking every part of him from every angle. I ran and punched my way there and felt pepper spray as I passed prison guards but bulldozed onward. I got to the youngster and started getting pummeled out in the open but still lifted him to his feet and dragged him twenty yards toward the opening of a building where more guards were and fell down.

After a few breaths I realized it was over and looked for Damon. He had followed me halfway and was lying on the ground painted orange from the pepper spray. I saw it dripping off his bullet shaped head and almost laughed through my own pain. I looked back at the youngster's scared face, it was swollen and bleeding but he'd be okay. I looked at our White table and saw Blockhead and Jason drenched in orange and found a bunch of other White inmates lying on their stomachs with their hands under them ready to pop back up if the Mexicans did. The Yard gate opened and an army of other prison guards from the other yards finally made it and for the first time I was glad to see them.

The army of prison guards stepped or knelt on White and Mexican inmates until the zip ties were placed on every wrist as handcuffs. I knew they would sort out who the actual combatants were in the Hole. I was lifted to my feet and met Damon and the others as we were corralled into a pile and escorted to the yard gate. It looked like all the Whites were okay other than some cuts and bruises.

We watched the yard gate open where dozens of prison guards from other yards were waiting to help with the escort. Over fifty prison guards dressed in green uniforms, that resembled military fatigues, positioned themselves on both sides of the single file line of inmates. Every prison guard was holding something. Some had 50 caliber rifles, others block guns and others held pepper spray canisters the size of a fire extinguisher. In contrast, the inmates all looked like tattooed down body builders and soldiers of a different ilk. The procession stretched for nearly 100 yards.

The experience felt eerie, almost out of body. As we walked I felt the pepper spray on the side of my face and neck eating deeper into my skin as it progressed down my body with my sweat, leaving a 'burned by fire' feeling in its wake. We walked by the second prison yard and through the razor wire fences saw over five hundred prisoners lying on the ground with prison guards walking amongst them holding guns at the ready in case our yard's riot kicked off another there. We passed that prison yard and I knew the inmates would remain on the ground in the prone position until we were housed in the Hole Administrative Segregation.

We walked another 500 yards and passed two more prison yards before reaching our destination. The Hole, Ad Seg, was behind the last yard in an isolated compound and we circled it. On the way that eerie feeling magnified with the noise. Men were training their bodies in a choreographed and precise manner. One leader was barking orders with the rest of the group responding, followed by the sounds of bodies exercising

and grunting. I began to make out the cadence, "Surenos!! Raza!! Estamos listos? Vamanos!" I knew enough Spanish prison slang to understand the cadence was being applied to the Southern California Mexicans and the Mexicans originally from Mexico, The Race, according to them and always at the ready to go.
Around the corner the building opened up enough to peer in at the portion the prisoners were allowed to use for yard two hours every other day. Instead of a regular prison yard, the prisoners were confined to kennels. Row after row of fenced in rectangular dog runs allowed two prisoners per cage 6' by 10' of width to pace back and forth or work out like they were now.
I realized something monumental. I had to find L'il Bird and Boxer, the two Mexicans labeled Mexican Mafia who were removed from the yard before the ensuing power struggle. I needed to communicate to them that the policy we had ironed out together hadn't been respected by Stranger, who stepped up to fill their void. Now that Stranger was gone from the yard, now in line with us to get processed into Ad Seg, the yard we just vacated was void of leadership again. Both L'il Bird and Boxer had the influence and reach to send word to that yard to keep the peace.
We turned the corner of the building again and were able to see the yard through the fence. I zeroed in on L'il Bird and Boxer. Their sturdy, older bodies stood out amongst the younger, less seasoned Mexicans. Both of their sweat glistened bodies were covered by tattoos blasted in aged ink from decades ago and fading. Both had collages of Aztec war scenes and I was hoping their power to command wasn't fading like the ink. I searched out the rest of the kennels and in the sea of Mexicans found four White men. The four Whites were distinguishable from the rest of the prisoners by their sheer size.
All four men had large bald heads and only one of them didn't have his scalp covered in tattoo ink to the forehead. That behemoth was the largest at 6'7" and at

least 280 lbs of iron clad frame. He was scrutinizing us with so much energy I couldn't look away. The eerie feeling magnified even more as I watched him focus on ascertaining why we were in line to get housed in Ad Seg with him, apparently his spot. He used his fingers for sign language and introduced his name, Bam Bam, his counterpart's name in the kennel with him, Blitz, along with Sinner and Traveler in the next kennel.

Next he used his fingers to ask us questions. "What prison yard had we just come from?" With our hands cuffed behind our backs in zip ties we had to communicate by nodding our heads or shaking them. He finger questioned, A-Yard? We shook our head no until he got to D-Yard. Then, he finger questioned, What happened with the Mexicans? His fingers were taking too long to go letter by letter so he resorted to mimicking possibilities that started with lifting a drink to his mouth to see if we had been drunk? We shook our heads no. He nailed it with his next one. He mimicked the act of registering a needle and shooting dope into his arm. We nodded our head vigorously that he was so warm he was in the oven with us. Next he lifted his hand and ran his fingers together in the universal sign for money and then used his hand to slide by his throat to say the money hadn't made it. We nodded our heads that he understood our problem. He then used his hand to make it look like he had a knife in it and jabbed it into his other hand repeatedly to ask if weapons were used. We shook our heads no. Then he used both of his fists to fire straight punches and we nodded our heads yes.

He went back to using his fingers to sign letter by letter and asked if the drug user that caused the problem was still on the yard. Even though Lefty had overdosed we nodded our heads that he was technically right. Time ran out to communicate because prison guards from the building walked into the yard and stopped next to Bam Bam's kennel. He didn't seem to mind the intrusion and finger signed to us that we were going to be housed in B-Pod.

Everyone heard a prison guard from the gun tower inside the building announce through a speaker, "Yard recall! Your two hours in the kennels are up! Kennels A and B, stand by for an escort to your cells."

For the next half hour we watched the kennels empty. One prisoner after another backed up and stuck both hands through a slot where a guard applied handcuffs to wrists. From there, we couldn't see the prisoners enter the building from our vantage point but heard a thick steel vestibule door creaking as it slid open. It closed with the last of the prisoners with a resounding thud.

The building in front of us was a prefabricated tan color. A thick steel green vestibule door creaked and grinded open as it slid on rollers. Above, a black tinted bullet proof window filled up with two prison gunners holding rifles. Right next to the window in red capital block letters read:

WARNING! NO WARNING SHOTS FIRED- C-6 ADMINISTRATIVE SEGREGATION.

The procession of prisoners proceeded in front of us and we shuffle stepped forward inch by inch. Being the last in line it took two hours to get to the vestibule door and inside the building. As we made it I looked up and saw the two prison gunners pointing their rifles at us as if we could get out from our cuffs and become a threat.

Shuffling through the vestibule door I kept looking up. We could see the gunners in the tower through a bullet proof plexiglass they walked on. A 4' by 8' square of plexiglass was constructed with a perforated opening to drop tear gas and fire the rifles through at us below. I heard the vestibule door behind us creak and slide shut and it felt like we were vacuumed into a dank and dark, all metal chamber of penal hell. I knew that a percentage of the prisoners living in these concrete corridors had been here for years and thought of Bam Bam, and wondered if he was one of them. We'd find out how things operated over here soon enough.

I looked back up at the tower through the plexiglass. From up there, the gunners had a vantage point that allowed access to each row of cell pods and I counted three rows facing west, three facing east and three facing north. The south quadrant covered the yard the prisoners had just come from. Each quadrant had a thick steel green vestibule door. Above each vestibule red block letters signified the location. I found A through C-Pod stamped over the west side quadrant and watched one of the tower gunners hit a switch on a command table and the vestibule opened.

From the gun tower we heard a guard yell out our names and which cells we were to be housed in.

"B-Pod Cell 123!"

"B-Pod Cell 122!"

I was glad to hear that Damon and I were in the same cell and that Blockhead and Jason were in the cell next to us. On the way there I noticed our bedrolls and new prison garb all wrapped up in a bundle with a couple of plastic spoons and cups parked in front of our cells.

The guard in the tower spoke instructions over the microphone, "When we take off the zip ties strip out of your clothes!"

We passed the first cell, a 6' wide by 10' long chamber of concrete. The cell door was made out of steel with perforated holes from top to bottom, inches away from each other making it hard to see in or out clearly. The cell door looked like honey comb. Inside the cell, two Blacks exercised and their silhouettes rose and fell as they took turns doing push-ups. I looked at the cell across from them and the same thing was happening with two more Black inmates. I assumed the Black and Asian inmates were getting their every other day yard tomorrow and were doing their exercises in the cell. We passed a few more cells and stopped at ours.

One of the four prison guards behind us said, "After we take the cuffs off strip down and let us search you. You know the drill."

I went first and got naked and waited for the instructions.

"Arms out wide...Arms up...Lift up your testicles...Turn around...Lift one foot and wiggle your toes...The other foot...Bend over and grab your ass cheeks and spread them...Now cough three times..."

Done with our strip search and locked up tight in our cell Damon let me take a bird bath first since I had more pepper spray on me. I filled up the sink attached to the toilet with water, then sat on the toilet facing the sink and splashed the water over my head with my cup. The water reignited the pepper spray and my eyes watered to ease the burning and I felt it in my lungs and started coughing.

Next to me Damon was taking one of his two pairs of boxer shorts apart. In the waist band of the boxers, after he pulled out the elastic, there was plenty of thread to weave together to turn it into a fishing line. He hooked three strands of thread to the cell door using the ventilated honey comb and went to the back of the cell and began weaving the thread into one line.

From outside our cell, on the tier about four cells down, we heard a prisoner yell, "Cell 122 and Cell 123! This is Traveler in Cell 118! I'm sending my line!"

While continuing my bird bath I watched Damon fastening together a small piece of soap into a piece of plastic until he had it attached to his newly woven fishing line. He crouched down on all fours and looked out the side of our cell and yelled, "Shoot it!"

A few minutes of successful fishing he pulled in a written note from Traveler and read it to me.

Greetings brothers:

Welcome to the catacombs. We saw you communicate with big Bam Bam and know you were involved in a riot with the Mexicans. Glad to see you're alright! I'm in the last cell in our B-Pod so I can get word to C-Pod when the prison guards open the door when they do the head count or pass out mail. I need you to send your paperwork as soon as possible to check you off the Roll Call list. Also, Bam Bam wants to know who ran up the drug debt? We get yard one day and showers the next with a day of zero program on Wednesday. On Wednesday the Prison Administration runs hearings. Speaking of hearings, that's when you will get checked to see how long you will be confined in here. For a riot they usually keep you for a couple of months if they have you involved in it in their reports. As soon as I get your paperwork I have a care package for you.

Damon scribbled off a note to let Traveler know what happened on our yard along with how Lefty had taken a back door exit by overdosing on heroin.

The next morning four prison guards arrived at our cell for an interview... The first guard, a very large and dark black man who had an experienced face with kind eyes, and had a nameplate on his chest that read: Jackson. Jackson seemed to be the leader of the four and I realized he was a Lieutenant. The other prison guard standing at the cell was of Mexican descent and a little younger. He wore an expression of impatience, nameplate: Torrez.

Jackson scrunched up close to the honeycomb cell door and said, "Inmate Smith and Johnson, also known as BJ, here is your paperwork for the riot. Now time to ask you some questions..."

We accepted the paperwork through the side of the cell door, and each of us took our time to read it. The top of the page had the form number, 114-D and next to it- Lock Up Order For Administrative Segregation. Underneath it started with the reason: Violation of Rule 123 "Group Melee." The report went on to read that the incident was a serious rule violation and for the safety and security of the prison we were deemed enemy combatants. The next paragraph had reports from prison guards who witnessed the riot from a gun tower and on the ground. I was glad to see that not one of the prison guards wrote who started the fight, just some of the inmates who were involved. It appeared that only fourteen inmates had pepper spray administered to their wardrobe. They were the only inmates considered, "Involved in the melee." It looked like the other thirty-

six inmates would get a reprieve and get "Kicked out" of Ad Seg and return to one of the other three prison yards soon.
Jackson started reading from the report...
"Inmate Smith and Johnson, you were both seen by tower guard Abadaco and Building 5 prison guard Jimenez as combatants involved in the riot and in their words 'Punching both fists repeatedly hundreds of times during the altercation hitting inmates Guerra, Alejandra, Sanchez, Lopez, Cordoba, Marquez, and inmate Delgado repeatedly'. The report goes on to say you were both pepper sprayed. This is the proof needed that you were both involved in the riot so you don't have much of a chance of beating the prison violations. Since weapons weren't used I don't think you have to worry about added charges with the District Attorney but these reports combined with your statements will be sent to them to see if the County wants to pick up additional charges. I don't think they will. None of the inmates had to get stitched up and there wasn't any great bodily injury other than some swelling and bruises and a little blood."
I stared at Lieutenant Jackson and appreciated his honesty. He was letting us in on the full impact and ramifications of the situation rather than letting us sweat out those pertinent details relating to the potential of outside charges with the District Attorney. He was also coaching us in that whatever we said would be used against us in reports. His Mexican partner Torrez, who I realized was a Sergeant, scared the shit out of us.
"We've looked at the video footage of the incident and it shows you as the aggressor BJ...If you don't cooperate with us we might have to write up the report to show that you instigated the riot. That will probably get the DA to pick up charges, plus we can raise the in-prison violation to a Level A charge..."
I knew the current charge we had read, "Group Melee", was a Level D charge in the California Prison Guide, also

known as the "Title 15". The most it carried as in prison punishment was up to nine months in Ad Seg as a SHU term. Sergeant Torrez was referring to a Level A charge usually reserved for Murder, Mayhem, Extortion, or a much more gray area, labeling a prisoner responsible for calling those shots by exerting pressure.
Both Damon and I stood there with stoic expressions on our faces, waiting...
Lieutenant Jackson started the questions. "What started the riot? We only want to know to see how long to keep the yard it happened on locked down." Neither Damon nor I spoke a word. We couldn't, the unwritten code of silence." Lieutenant Jackson nodded his head that he understood our predicament and wrote down and said, "No comment."
Sergeant Torrez looked angry. His face contorted into that impatient frustrated look he brought originally. He said, "We know it was over dope. Did your race or you, BJ, do more dope than you could pay for and then decide the best way out was to get in a fight to get off the yard?"
I knew he was baiting me and it almost worked. I wanted to tell them that yeah it was over dope. Lefty saw half the Mexicans on the yard nodding off and scratching their bodies, high as fuck on heroin. His drug addicted diseased mind was jealous and the desire to use that heroin and get as fucked up as half the Mexicans pushed him past the point. Not that I was excusing his actions. But I was questioning how Termite was smuggling enough heroin into our prison to get two hundred Mexicans so high that they were throwing up all over the yard. Was a prison guard helping him smuggle it? I couldn't imagine how through monitored visits with cameras everywhere, that much heroin could slip through. Usually, smaller amounts made it by the visitor kissing a small balloon of packaged drugs across with it being swallowed by the prisoner and thrown up later...

I finally responded, "It was no big deal. That was a cheer leader fight. All we did is wave some pom-poms around. You can open the yard back up over there..." I knew they wouldn't open up the yard for a minimum of two weeks. They would follow protocol and sweep the yard for weapons and a few other things first. I'd have time to contact L'il Bird and Boxer and restore peace...Hopefully.

Sergeant Torrez scribbled in his report with an angry face and I looked at Lieutenant Jackson. He noticed my worried expression and shook his head as if to say, everything will be alright.

Sergeant Torrez looked like he was trying to scrunch his face up into something intimidating. He looked at me as hard as he could and said, "BJ, you're parole date is tomorrow. Why in the fuck did you get involved in this? Now you might not go home, unless you tell me what I need to know! What exactly happened over there so we can investigate the riot properly?"

I looked at the Sergeant for a while and finally said, "No comment." I wanted to tell him that if I helped him by talking he would have to write it in a report that would then come back to us, that we would then have to carry with us and pass along to other prisoners. That would be another security threat because we weren't supposed to talk about those kinds of things. Just because my parole date was set for tomorrow it wasn't time to become a rat.

The Sergeant said, "Last chance to work with me and possibly go home tomorrow..." "No comment."

Lieutenant Jackson smiled at us like we did what we were supposed to do. He knew the program and was just doing his job. He said, "We're going to run showers for the Whites and Mexicans after we release the Blacks and Asians to the yard kennels. After that we have to take you two out of the cell for some pictures and some more questions about gang affiliation."

Damon and I both said in unison, "No comment."

A half hour later we heard cell doors pop open. We looked out the cell and saw Traveler and Sinner come out of their cell with towels and shower supplies. They came right to our cell and filled us in.

Traveler was as tall as Damon at 6'3", with a shredded bulletproof build. He said, "We heard that interview, good job with the no comment. BJ if your parole date is tomorrow you might have to stay a few extra days but you will go home. Take this Title 15 and read it. The state can't keep you indefinitely for a riot unless there is good cause for the District Attorney to charge you with a new beef. Since weapons weren't used you're out of here. L'il Bird and Boxer are already on top of things and they got at us to tell you they send their respects and regards and to not worry about the yard you just left. They're sending Cyclone back to take control of the yard for the Mexicans and the policy you guys already had in place is going to stay the same. The only thing they want is for Lefty to get dealt with..."

The first thing I thought was that it was a good thing I spoke loud enough to Stranger for Cyclone and Termite to hear before the riot. They must have heard, or already knew, the drug policy we had worked out was being violated. The second thing I thought, thank God they were handling their business so honorably.

We handed our Lock Up Order 114-D paperwork to Traveler to follow protocol and he slid us a sack of goodies that included some prison store food, toiletries and some writing paper and stamped envelopes. Sinner had a handful of books for us to read to help kill the time stuck in our cell almost 24-7 in slow motion. I had to ask, "How long have you guys been here?"

Traveler said, "Bam Bam has been here the longest at two years and two months. They're determining if he's going to Pelican Bay as a validated mobster. He wanted us to warn you that this prison seems to want these cells in Ad Seg filled. They're on a fishing expedition to validate as many prisoners as shot callers as possible. My cellie and I have been here for a year and a half for defending ourselves in a riot outnumbered 20 to us 2. With such bad odds we both had weapons in our hands. The weapons have us screwed. What did they want us to do, just let them kill us?"

We watched Traveler and Sinner leave our cell and heard their cell door shut. A couple of minutes later we heard the vestibule open and we got some more visitors. Sergeant Torrez crowded our cell door with a smirk on his face with six IGI Gooners behind him. We called the Inmate Gang Investigators Gooners because they wore similar uniforms to the regular prison guards but had additional black stitching on their shoulders and chest that resembled tattoos to signify they were in charge of deciphering who the gangsters were, usually based on their tattoos.

We backed up to the cell door one at a time and stuck our wrists through the slot to accept the handcuffs. After we backed out of the cell we had one IGI Gooner on each side of us holding our shoulders to steer our direction. Sergeant Torrez led the way and just as we got to Traveler and Sinner's cell he said, "Time to take some pictures of you to add to the gang file and have an interview out of hearing so you can really open up to us."

I knew he was trying to stir the pot and make it look like we might yap our gums and talk. They were always trying to play the divide and conquer game to keep the prisoners fighting each other instead of uniting for a common cause, like finding a new life away from prison walls...

We stopped at an office and there were two other IGI Gooners inside with cameras and a table full of files next to them. Sergeant Torrez grabbed our files off the desk and handed them over. I read the nameplate from the first Gooner's shoulder to receive our files, Velazquez, and noticed he was listed as a Lieutenant. The other Gooner to get our files was Perez, another Lieutenant.

Sergeant Torrez looked at us like a bully and said, "Strip down to nothing. It's time to take some pictures to beef up your files. Let's see those tattoos."

I knew I would disappoint this branch of fault finders. I didn't have any tattoos. Damon on the other hand was a sculpted banner of ink. They were going to have a field day with him.

I stripped down and stared at Sergeant Torrez. He looked even more frustrated. He said, "Turn around BJ."

I turned around and heard him say, "Not one tattoo BJ? What's wrong with you? Every other prisoner has tattoos. How do you have so much influence without them?"

I responded, "Who said I have influence? If I have any it's because I'm not trendy."

I heard Sergeant Torrez whistle and say, "Look at all that ink on Smith. We should be able to label some of that ink as gang affiliated."

"Turn around Smith"

Damon turned around and looked at me with a sour expression on his face and I whispered, "Don't say anything."

We heard Sergeant Torrez pull one of the Inmate Gang Investigators aside and close the office door behind them. We listened and barely heard the Sergeant say, "We can put everything on Smith and write it up that he was the shot caller that provoked the riot..."

We heard the IGI Gooner respond, "Yeah, I like that. With all of those prison tattoos we can write it up that he's part of a prison gang and a leader. We should be able to keep him housed in Ad Seg until the Pelican Bay SHU has an opening..."

The door opened and they walked back inside. "Turn around."

We turned around and I studied Sergeant Torrez. I was starting to hate him. He was a power tripper who was willing to do whatever it took to screw people like us. He grabbed one of the cameras and got close enough to

Damon's naked body for it to feel weird. The feeling intensified because his face took on a glow, like he was getting off on the process. With his face six inches away from Damon's stomach he asked, "What does Rott stand for? Is that you're AKA?"

Damon didn't say anything...

"What about that banner of ink flowing across your chest with the Ace of Spades flying off the table with the dice? Does that mean you control the gambling in here?"

Damon remained silent...

"What about the 737 on your shoulder, what does that stand for?" Lieutenant Inmate Gang Investigator Perez came closer with an excited look on his face. "That's a gang tattoo! I know I have it in my files somewhere." The energy increased with Perez's excitement and the questions came in rapid fire.

"What do they call you besides BJ?"

"What do they call you Smith?"

"Who do you run with?"

"What gang are you from?"

"What neighborhood do you represent?"

"Are you affiliated with the Aryan Brotherhood?"

"How about the Nazi Low Riders?"

"Are you Skin Heads? Are you Peckerwoods? Come on I know you're someone!" The feeling of doom intensified as the reports were scribbled faster along with the flashing lights from the cameras. It felt like we were on an out of control train about to get derailed.

Inmate Gang Investigator Torrez flipped the pages in his gang file and with excitement that bordered on glee, said, "See, right here! Look at the tattoo on this inmate... He has the number 737 tattooed on his shoulder also. When we interrogated him he admitted his AKA is Casper and also admitted his gang affiliation as OCS, short for Orange County Skin Head. He also told us the structure of White gang leadership in prison starts with the Aryan Brotherhood dominating the Nazi Low Riders, who dominate the Skin Head gangs. He said a Roll Call list is taken on every prison yard in California to organize the power structure..."

On the walk back to our cells we passed Traveler and Sinner standing at their cell door watching. I remembered Traveler's warning about the fishing expedition. It felt like we'd just been hooked and thrown all over the place. But where were we going to land? It felt hard to breath, like a fish out of water...

The next morning started with Sergeant Torrez. He stood in front of the cell smiling at us looking smug, like he had won the war. He had some papers in his hand and said, "Here's some more paperwork related to the riot you caused Smith, or should I call you by your AKA, Rott?"

I pulled the reports through the side of the cell and realized what was happening. They'd decided to focus on Damon because they didn't have time to focus on me since the DA wouldn't pick up the charges and keep me from making my parole date. I'd be going home within five days according to the Title 15. With me gone, I wouldn't be able to be a witness for Damon that he didn't coerce me into doing what I did...

Sergeant Torrez took one last parting shot with, "If you would have cooperated with me you wouldn't be in this mess. I could have saved your ass from living in solitary. It still might not be too late.... If you give me enough good information about the gangs in here, I still might be able to help you avoid this hole for the rest of your life."

I knew I was going home and leaving Damon to this fate. He still had three years left on his sentence and it looked like it might be spent in isolation. I looked at him and watched him say, "No comment."

A couple hours later Lieutenant Jackson showed up. He also had reports. He handed them through the side of the cell. We took our time reading them and found the Lieutenant had investigated more thoroughly and found the truth and defended us, somewhat. We listened to him say the same thing that we were reading...

"I pretty much know with certainty what happened over there to cause that riot. The Mexicans were without any leadership and there were too many chiefs and not enough Indians. Also, somehow, there was enough heroin on the yard to kill a hundred people. From there it doesn't take a rocket scientist to figure out that the White inmate who overdosed ran up a drug debt. I also know that a year ago on the same yard the Whites were attacked in a riot that sent sixteen Whites to the infirmary on stretchers. It was over a drug debt. You guys were probably just protecting yourselves the best you knew how. I've been around these California prison corridors for thirty years and I know it's just a system of warehouses filled with mostly drug addicts and alcoholics. I don't like what Sergeant Torrez is doing to you Smith. He wants to become an Inmate Gang Investigator and his passion to do so pushes him too far."

It was nice to hear but was it and the report enough to help Damon? Probably not.

Lieutenant Jackson shook his head and kept being honest. "BJ, you're going home tomorrow. Smith you're going to be stuck in this cell, in isolation for at least three months while the investigation proceeds. You will probably do the rest of your sentence in here and Pelican Bay while the Administration decides if they can validate you as a prison gang leader. Make the best of it and good luck.

Want more? You can contact Glenn Langohr via email: rollcallthebook@gmail.com

Author Page: http://www.amazon.com/-/e/B00571NY5A

Author Page UK: http://www.amazon.co.uk/-/e/B00571NY5A

Blog: http://rollcallthebook.blogspot.com/

Smashwords: http://www.smashwords.com/profile/view/lockdownpublishing.com

Facebook Pages:
https://www.facebook.com/glennlangohrcalifornia
https://www.facebook.com/lockdownpublishingdotcom
https://www.facebook.com/KindlePrisonStories
Twitter: https://twitter.com/#!/rollcallthebook

CPSIA information can be obtained
at www.ICGtesting.com
Printed in the USA
FSOW04n2016111217
42321FS